FIRST TO FINISH; LAST TO WIN

Chasing the Ghost

Clarence CJ Jones

To my brothers, Larry, Dexter, Stanley, Christopher, & Ronald thank you for allowing me to watch You to become ME! Words could never express how Much I admire you all and I hope by dedicating my first book.

To you all will help me say Thank You for allowing me To watch your hard-work, character, enthusiasm, Personalities, and sense of humour. You all created. A GIANT and I will always carry you all in my heart along with me.

Thank you,

I Love you.

Acknowledgements

In life there is always a moment that life makes you realize that it is time to stand up and be a man. This moment doesn't come with bells and whistles. Most of all this moment does not come with instructions or pictures to see if you are getting it right. My moment came when I met two young boys by the name of Marquis and Anthony. Meeting them helped me grow, it made me realize that I did not have all the answers and that I could screw some things up royally. Meeting them made me realize that I was not Superman and that all the awards, accolades, and acknowledgements was a smoke screen to what life is about. They challenged me in ways that I never imagined, and they have also made me proud in ways that I never thought. I want to thank these young boys, now young men, for giving me the opportunity to be a dad. Even though it was the first time that I wasn't good at something, they made me look at me and to realize my shortcomings. Without them I probably would have never known my shortcomings, without them I would not have realized the importance of raising young men with character, honesty, respect, and empathy, without them First to Last, Last to Finish would have never been finished. You both have motivated me to do better when I have not always done right. You all have allowed me to be a better father to my daughter, your sister, because of the mistakes I made with you. Thank you both for making me realize that what is important has nothing to do with being right, but with being consistent and finishing what you started. This book is a long time coming and because you two came in my life it forced me to be a better man. This book is for all the men that struggle with life biggest challenges and refuse to heal the scars and wounds that we hide daily. First to Finish; Last to Win is for all the black men that get up every day to Win!

Table of Contents

CJ-ism #29 – *You may be small in man's eye, but you are a giant in God's eye. This world is too small, there is nothing that you cannot conquer!*

Preface

As we packed up from the polling place, I knew we had won. The number of people that had showed up to vote and with the demographics, it was inevitable that a win would be the outcome. After a couple months of canvasing, setting up interviews, having meetings, and wondering if we were on the right course, somehow there was a sense of excitement and a sense of disappointment. This had been the story of my life. Use your ability, your knowledge, and your skills to help someone else succeed at a dream you shared, but in some awkward way, you would never get the true feeling of the success. It would only be felt through another individual, company, or group.

This book is not to blame anyone for their successes. It is not to regret extending the hand to help anyone succeed. This book is strictly for healing. Healing is probably one of the hardest things to do. As I navigate through these pages, at the end of this journey, prayerfully it is wished that healing takes place for me as an author and as the reader.

I am a dreamer. My dreams are real and the only things stopping my dreams is fear. Fear is my doubts telling my dreams that anything that my mind is set to accomplish cannot be done. However today I will step outside the box. Stepping out of the box is necessary because my foundation is strong. Inevitably my foundation will be the norm so today I am preparing myself to take my first step outside the box.

Foreword

Many times, we talk with the intention that everything that we say people are listening to us. There are times when I find myself talking whether it's with my family, co-workers, or friends and then realize that they have stopped listening to what was being said. As people we must realize that just because we want to say something does not mean that we have to say it. One of my sayings comes from people saying, "Say what you mean and mean what you say." I like to say, "Know what you are saying and know when to say it." We all have important things to say, but if every time we speak, we are rumbling and what we say have little substance people will begin to tune us out. So just because you are talking; does not mean anyone is listening!

Shut Your Black Ass Mouth! Many may see this as a joke but to me this statement is a lesson learned. Growing up there was no voice. There was not any reference of being heard, only being seen. Being seen was not always in the brightest of lights. Going from a young kid with no voice, to a man that everyone expects you to have an opinion can be a gift and a curse. Life was so much easier being in the background. This was learned earlier in my days as a young Airman in the United States Air Force. Leaving North Carolina was the beginning of something different. As a freshman at St. Augustine's College, it was a feeling that a grown man decision had to be made about my future. Mad at my mother because she did not give me money to go shopping for clothes, I walked to the recruiter station and enlisted into the military. "Are you sure this is what you want to do," said the recruiter? He seemed as if he was skeptical. A slim shy black kid coming into his office, walking with no parents, and could not give one reason why he wanted to join the military. I said, "Yes, I think at this time, this is what is best for me. I need my own money." He looked and was like, "I want you to take a math practice test." He was basically saying I am not going to waste my time on you if you are not able to pass this practice test. You can go over and talk to the Marines or the Army. He didn't know that the Army was my first choice. That decision was derailed by my brother who was prior Army. So, he gave me the practice math test and answered eight of the ten problems correctly. Me gloating, I stated, "My major in college is Mathematical Education. I am not here because I am failing school. My GPA is 3.6. I am here because I want my own money." This may have been the beginning of me needing to Shut My Black Ass Mouth. After that the recruiter set me up with taking an ASVAB test and within two weeks, the test was taken, a job was selected. I had a date to leave for the United States Air Force on March 17, 1992. This grown man decision was paying off. After several walks from the campus to the recruiter's station, I was finally checking out of school. As quickly, as I had in processed for the semester, it was even quicker to out-process. However, during the out process there was one lady that said, "you are out processing. You wasted a space for someone else." This was the first time that the realization of me not using my voice came to pass. In my mind a full conversation was going on. My thoughts were, "What do you mean I am wasting a spot. I have a 3.6 GPA and cannot get a job on campus to work, while we have students with 2.0 GPAs that you are treating like kings. Who are you to tell me I am wasting a spot when you do not know why I am leaving? Instead of saying I am wasting a spot how about asking me why I am withdrawing as soon as I in-processed. How about seeing if there is anything you can do to help or keep me in the institution instead of offering your criticism." This scenario has always played back in my head as to why was nothing said and why was it so hard to express myself. Through the year's things have gotten better, but through this journey of being able to express my thoughts. There are some lessons learned.

One lessoned learned is that no one really wants your opinion unless they want your opinion. In life we all have a moral compass, and it is believed by me that with this moral compass we have seconds maybe longer to decide on an action. To decide on whether we feel the decision is right or wrong. This does not mean that the decision is right or wrong in the situation, but however right or wrong morally. So, when offering advice there are two areas that the person giving the opinion or advice must be able to navigate. Those areas are morally and consciously or in the flesh. In many situations there has been a struggle for me to make these decisions and often give advice to myself or other people. As a young Airman there are many decisions that were made that should have never been made. Starting my military career, you could have called me the stellar airman. As an E-1 in the military and overseeing your own shop was unheard of during that time. With the great training and mentoring of a Senior Airman Fuller, it allowed me to be the primary supply technician of the Isochronal Dock for C-141 aircraft. There was rarely a chance that I worked a complete day. After that experience, my next job was in MICAP and Stock Control. Two of the best supervisors I ever had Sgt Flippin and Sgt Martin was there and there was something about that office. They instilled a confidence in me that made me feel like I belong. It was a cockiness that was needed but not arrogant. It was a confidence that said, "If You Know, You Know and Don't Let Anyone Tell You Different." Stock Control was a privilege to work. Everyone did not just work in Stock Control. You were in the big times in that office. Even though, this was the cream of the crop this was the point where my career started to change. Nothing drastic happened, it was a time when the clash of moral decisions and fleshly decisions began to alter my whole existence.

Awards was nothing new. There was Honor Guard and Below-the-Zone awards to receive my E-4 ranking. Everyone knew Airman Jones was smart and sharp, whether you liked me or not. That was something that you could not take away. Then one day there was a call from the man that saved my career, this first time. There were a few times my military career was on the line. Making it twenty years was not a crystal stair for me. So, MSgt Petty calls me while I am on an honor guard detail and he says, "Where are you?" I let him know, "I am on the way back from doing a funeral detail." His next words were, "Don't come to work, you have the Sheriffs at the job looking for you." Everything started running through my head, then he let me know that there were bad checks written by me. The sheriffs were there to collect me or the money. He spoke with the sheriffs and told them that he would make sure that a visit would be made by me to the South Carolina Law Enforcement Department to settle or make arrangement to pay my debts. How he was able to keep this out of the First Sergeants office is a miracle to me, but this would not be the first time he saved me from myself.

All of this stemmed from not making the right decisions. It was the realization that taught me after I played everything back, that there was that second or more window for me to say this is right or this is wrong. However, in the flesh, this was the right decision to make because of my circumstances in my mind. The reason they were looking for me was because there was over three hundred dollars in bad checks written to BI-LO for grocery. At the time as a member of honor guard we received a basic allowance for food. We could not eat in the dining facility because it was a perk, we received for being on honor guard. For so many years none of my decisions had come back to really make me face reality. This decision allowed everything to be put in perspective. To try to instantly fix the situation, a call home was placed to my mom to ask if she had three hundred dollars until payday. She said she did not have it. Then it was asked if she could ask my brother if he had it, she said no again. Never telling her what the money would be used for instantly it upset me, and a vow was made that asking people for anything would not happen again. My bad decision set the tone for being stubborn and not asking anyone for help, even when it was needed, regardless of the help. After coming to the realization that I would have to go to the Sherriff Office with no money in my pocket, that Monday morning the trek was made.

Driving up to the SLED office seemed to be so dismal, even though it was a workday it seemed the only car was mine and I was on my way to either cut a deal or be put in jail for three hundred dollars. Not only three hundred, but three hundred that my mom would not give me to keep her son out of jail. I had made it personal. It was no longer about my bad decision but was about why my mom didn't help me. I could not believe that she did not have the money, I made myself believe she just did not want to give it to me. This became a strain for me and hindered my relationship with my mother. It wasn't about her saying no, but more about a letter that was written to me by my mother while training in technical school.

At this point in my life, I started listening, even if no one was speaking. The idea of what people thought about me came from within myself and those thoughts became the interpretation of what in my mind people thought of me. If you are listening, this book will take you on a journey of a man that navigated life feeling that he was not good enough. However, he survived, he accomplished, and he saw things that many grew up with him didn't. Yet, it was still not enough for the race he is running. A race that requires a balance of speaking, being quiet, giving a soft response, and cursing some people the fuck out! Once I arrived at the SLED office, I spoke to the Sheriff, and they decided I would pay $50 dollars every two weeks until the debt was paid. It was a painful lesson but with easy solution. In that instance, I thought I had won, however at what cost. My painful battle with money and my idea of winning had just begun.

Loving yourself, how do you love yourself when there is nothing about yourself that you love? For years growing up the hardest thing was to love myself. There was nothing to love, about being dark, crooked teeth, and not the best eye candy in the store. So how could loving myself be an option? These thoughts made it hard to believe that one could be loveable. Throughout high school some days were good; some were bad it's still hard not to remember being called Ebae (from Good Times). A lot of my friends were females, but why were they, my friends is something that I would always think. It was never because they were genuine friends but wanting to think it was for some other reason always crossed my mind. In my mind, this dark skin was a curse. It was the beginning of all jokes, if was the catalyst of my insecurities, and it was the reason why no one could just be friends with me for whom I was as an individual. Not until senior year of senior superlatives did the realization that people liked me. Friendliest, Most School Spirited, and Most Popular were the categories that my peers bestowed upon me. Why did that matter? It mattered because for the first time it said that I had been accepted. Those wins were accepted, and college would be the next opportunity for me to step outside of the box on the way to my life's journey.

Stepping out of the box was a representation or symbol of leaving Franklinton, the shyness, succeeding and becoming a man. The box for me was being in Franklinton, comfort and the shyness and experience of being born in a family of ten being the youngest. There was not much expectation but knowing there was something better is what has always given me the strength to keep pushing. Knowing that there was something better was instilled in me at an early age. Whether it was done intentionally or done out of love was never the question. The question has always been, "Do they know how they impacted my life?" During the summers I would spend time with my cousin. My brother and his mom would take us somewhere every year, Kings Dominion, Busch Gardens, etc. For me it was not about the amusement parks, but it was more about the travel to the parks. We would leave early in the mornings and as we drove to this far off place, in my mind, we would see the sunrise and set sometimes while driving. As a young kid the journey to Virginia seemed far away from North Carolina. This was my first thought of thinking that there was something bigger outside of the box. The possibilities, the excitement, and the beginning of chasing the ghost at an early age. This brick that was given to me by them was the cornerstone of my foundation of the three pillars of my life that I feel is vital to succeed in life. The first pillar is relationship. This includes relationship with God, self, parents, family, friends, and even in networking. The second pillar is determination. Determination to do more, be more, and see more. A determination that says quitting is not an option and you must succeed or die. Finally, Success! The Ghost that cannot be contained. Chasing the ghost takes you through a life full of emotions and it put me on a race in life that I don't know if I will ever get the final win.

The journey of this book "First to Finish…Last to Win" is all about Clarence Jones chasing a ghost. Chasing a ghost of success, chasing a ghost to be loved, chasing a ghost to be healed, and finally chasing a ghost to Win. I learned that you would have many firsts in your life. You can be the first to finish college. You can be the first to own a home. You can be the first become President. Through all these accomplishments, you can also be the Last to Win! Chasing the ghost doesn't allow you to win, it allows you to finish. However, you can't win because our ghost keeps changing. First to Finish... Last to Win! I want to win one day!

CJ-ism #26 – *Some of the hardest wounds to heal are the wounds without scars!*

RELATIONSHIPS

CJ-ism # 21 - *Something to think about... "Men are we aware that as the "HEAD OF THE HOUSEHOLD" nothing comes in our homes except through US?... a lot to swallow but think about things that happen at home and then think about what we do or are doing and how it has an impact...*

Chapter 1: It's Just A Little Lie

Relationship conversations with my father: Conversation One: "You know if you suck the right tit, you will make the left one jealous. Conversation Two: Why do you keep pissing in bed? You are not going to be anything but a little faggot pissing in the bed every night. Conversation Three: What in the world do you mean to tell me she ran over here just to kiss you in the mouth? I have been trying to get her over here in the house ever since she moved back in with her mother. These can be called conversations, but when it comes to relationship advice, this is all that was given. As you may tell from these three conversations, I spent a lot of time trying to make a tittie jealous while avoiding homosexuality and trying to show everyone who would look and listen that I was the man. Being a man for me has always been about acceptance. Not until later did I learn that being a man has nothing to do with intercourse with women, acceptance by the guys, or being talked about for your escapades. Many nights, I have slept with women and felt the emptiness that can't be described.

There have been beautiful women and ugly women. There have been black women and white women. There have been Asian women and Latino women. Tall and short women, big and small women and of all these women, it has only been two that I have been in love with. Two that I loved and two I wanted to love, but I knew I would hurt them.

Relationships started to become awkward for me. It started in the Academy Village projects on the hood of a car with a group of people older teenagers and my younger friends saying, "Kiss her, kiss her, kiss her." Not the ideal situation but this was my introduction to "women." It goes without saying that I was scared, and my cousin ended up kissing her to supposedly show me that its nothing scary about getting a kiss. She went on to say she did not want to be my girlfriend and I cried listening to Is This the End by New Edition. That would be my last encounter with a "girlfriend" until I graduated high school. Today's world is totally different from the world we live in today. In my opinion, social media has exposed children to more than what we were ever exposed to as children.

Even though what we did then was no different than what is done now, the only saving grace was we did not have cameras. Sex was never readily available to me growing up and having a relationship was out of the picture until after graduation and I really learned what true love was supposed to look like in a romantic situation. With her, I chased her until she got tired, I guess. It was day one a young girl was in my homeroom class, very quiet. Instantly, I knew that I liked her and wanted to be her boyfriend. Away I went writing the love letters, *do you love me? I want to be your boyfriend; will you be my girlfriend?* This went on for a couple of weeks and a couple of letters. Then, I received an emphatic answer that nearly changed my world. "NO," she said. I stood in the hall, and she stood in the hall like is there any more question? There wasn't, for that day at least. What I found out was someone else was interested in her. It was one of my best friends. When that was found out the feeling of defeat did not hurt that bad. There wasn't any anger. It was more of like a calmness that said okay, he is cool. Go about your business. It didn't change the way I felt about her, but I settled for the friendship which stood the test of time. This cat-and-mouse game went on for the next four years of school. We became great friends and she and other mutual friends would come to my house, and it was one of the most important relationships in my life. I loved her! We continued to communicate and even during high school, we worked at Burger King, and she would pick me up for work. We laughed as if we were together. I knew when she was upset, I knew when she was happy, and I knew when she needed to be hugged. One of the complicated issues in this relationship was she was a Jehovah's Witness. Some of her hardest battles were between me and her faith. We were friends because our relationship was not approved by her father. She loved her father and I understood. When she finally said that she wanted us to be in a relationship, I asked what about your father and what about you and your standing at the Kingdom Hall. She said, "I can't help who I love!" She was my everything. I didn't and never had much money, but that was never an issue for us. We enjoyed each other or spoke with each other daily. Even when I went off to college, she would visit and sneak up to the dorm with our other friend that she always hung with during those days. We enjoyed each other. Before I left for the military, we broke up. I don't remember there being an argument, but I do remember she started dating someone from the Kingdom Hall. He was a handsome young fellow. Christopher Williams brown skin, Al B Sure hair, and his family had a car business that afforded him transportation I did not have. They went on to be married, but it did not stop the love we had for each other. I understood why she married him, and I do believe that she loved him. However, I never believed she loved him as much as she loved me. Sporadically, we would speak as friends while she was married. If I came home and she had time, she may stop by to see me. However, we both knew she was married, and we respected her situation.

In life, there have been decisions made that if the chance were to arise again, even though my heart says to make a different decision, I believe I made the right decision. This scenario has happened three times in my life. The first was with the love of my life. One weekend, while home visiting from the military, we met at her place. She and one of my best friends were roommates. This was the week before she was to get married. The three of us laughed and talked and before leaving, we had time to spend together and talk. She reminded me that she was getting married. I said I know. She said if you don't want me to get married, all you have to do is tell me not to get married and I will not marry him. We went back and forth because I said if you don't want to get married, do not marry him. This cannot be my decision. You must make that decision for yourself. We talked and cried in each other's arms that night. I knew the lady I loved would be married and, in my mind, I thought that she didn't think the man she loved loved her enough. A few months after the wedding, we connected and would continue to connect throughout the years through telephone calls. The last time I physically saw her was one day she visited my sister's house while I was home visiting. We caught up and she was smiling as always. Knowing her for so many years, I knew she was not happy but content. We shared some feelings and regrets and she left. Continuing to speak on the phone, she called me one day and she said, "I wrote you a letter. However, I am scared to send it. It's in my closet so that it will not be found by my husband, but I wrote it and one day I will give it to you." This was a happy day in her life; she was starting a new job, and she was approved for adoption of a young child. We spoke and at this point, I was happy that she was happy.

That night, for some reason, I could not sleep. I tossed and turned and then, in the middle of the night, my chest started to hurt for about 10 to 15 seconds and then stopped suddenly. There was no thought of anything strange, but after it, I went to sleep. The next morning at work, my sister called. She told me that she had passed away last night. I was in complete shock. It was complete disbelief because we had spoken the day prior. Quickly, I informed my supervisor. He knew if I was upset, she was someone special. He told management that my fiancé had passed away and I needed to leave. Even though she was not my fiancé, the sound of it felt good and from that point on, that is who she was to me. Driving home, I did not believe she had passed. That is one drive from Charleston, SC and remembering to cross the SC border was vague. The drive home was on autopilot from the time I left the base. Once I arrived home, one of my friends met me before I got out of the car. He didn't say a word; I couldn't do anything but cry on his shoulder. Reality set in my mind. She was gone. Later, I found out she passed away late at night and early morning, and to this day, no one can tell me differently that our connection was so close that I felt her leave. After getting myself together, I made the track to her home to pay my condolences. When I arrived, I asked to speak with her husband. He saw me and took me into their bedroom. He told me that she was going to start a job today and that they were supposed to adopt a young child. He told me how happy she was, and he could not believe that she was gone. I knew all of this, but I sat and listened. Then he turned to me, and he said, "She always loved you and I knew it." He further added, "She never loved me the way that she loved you." I stopped him and I told him she loved you. I know she did. This is a time for grieving. This is not the time to talk about whom she loved. We agreed to talk again after the funeral, and I left. Leaving, I knew I would never speak to him again. I felt a lot of different emotions. That I was robbed of true love, that I should have told her not to marry him, that she would still be alive if she was with me, and finally, I felt sorry for him to know that she loved another man and to feel that she never loved you as she loved me. The letter she wrote, I never received, but I am convinced that his thoughts were confirmed. There are still days that the thoughts of her go through my mind and if they never leave, I am fine with that also.

After the loss of my love, things began to get wild for me. One of the stigmas that I had in the military was that I was the man. However, most of it was just talk. There were a lot of women, many of them were friends and I did not sleep with them all. It was an awkward time because most of my friends had moved off base, but I stayed in the dorm. Not for the girls, but I was scared to move off. I had never managed money, bills, or lived alone. *How would I survive in an apartment?* I stayed with what I was comfortable with. That was the dorm. One of my turning points in life was Jungle Fever and the emergence of Wesley Snipes. Growing up, the dark man was not sexy, wanted, or even considered a sex symbol. I'm not saying I was all of this, but for the first time, this is the way I felt. There were escapades at the base park, downtown on the Charleston Battery, the making of sex VCR tapes, in the warehouse while working at night, running through base housing trying not to be seen at married women's homes, and leaving at night late night not to be seen visiting other people dorm rooms. The funny part of all of this is I still had no game. Many of the women I met basically knew me before I knew them. Some would come up and say, *oh, you are CJ. I heard about you.* When I asked what they heard, they would say to watch out for you because you are slick and that you would be trying to talk with me. It was hilarious, most of the haters did the work for me. This would go on at every base where I was stationed. It went

14

on in South Carolina, South Korea, and North Carolina. I was indirectly the man without being the man. It was all love for me and there were even times that I would go in to work and guys would come by the job to see who the dragon slayer had slayed. In my mind, I was catching up from being the little black boy that no one wanted to go to school to the young man who had a pick of ladies. Wesley Snipes did that for me as I laughed in my mind. He will always be the one that changed my life. In the military, being with women was never really an issue, but being with a lot of women can be the loneliest time in a person's life. There was no fulfillment. It was getting old. I looked back and thought, *is this all it's going to be? Not until one day that a joke turned into me finding my second true love. My wife!*

I was in Fayetteville NC I had it all. I had a car, my own place and women whenever I wanted them, and I had to answer to no one. *The LIFE!* So, I thought, *One night I was sitting in my living room, and I was thinking, I have no complaints, but why am I so lonely? I wanted to know why I am sitting here lonely when I have it all. Does anyone love me?* At that moment, a voice said to me, "YOU DON'T LOVE YOURSELF!" I stopped and thought that it was crazy. I knew I wasn't drunk because I did not drink anymore, so I was like I am just imagining things. Then I heard it again, "YOU DON'T LOVE YOURSELF!" At that point, I went to the mirror, and I did not see a person that I loved. That night, I cried because I realized I was not doing all these things for myself. I was doing them because I did not love myself. I could not find one thing about myself that I loved. It was as if everything had been taken off and the only thing left there was me, naked and transparent and I had to realize that I did not love myself. So, what was life to me?

From that point on, I made it a point to try to find something about myself daily until I learned to love myself. Sometimes, I would say you have a pretty smile, even though I knew I had crooked teeth, but I kept saying it until I believed it and when I doubted, I said it more. After weeks of this, I came to the realization that I live by today. Love yourself before you try to love anyone else because if you do not love yourself, who will? How can you love anyone else if you don't love yourself and make yourself happy before you try to make anyone else happy? When you are not happy, there is no way you can make anyone else happy. I started to live by it, I started to do it, and I started to believe it. When I looked in the mirror, I saw someone I loved and I knew regardless of how the day went, when I returned home, there was someone in the mirror who loved me. After I was comfortable with it, I found someone else who loved me, MY WIFE!

Relationships are vital to everyday life. Not until I got older did I realize that every relationship you are in has a direct influence from something that has happened in your past, whether it is a friendship, intimate relationship, marriage, co-worker relationship, or a relationship with complete strangers. Being in all these relationships, one of the hardest relationships to be in is marriage. I have found out that this is not just the hardest relationship for me but for every man who is in a marriage or intimate relationship. A lot of times, we as men, especially black men, get a hard time for being dogs, deadbeat fathers, no good and a few more adjectives that I could go on and on describing. As I sit here and think about me, my boys, our relationships, I wonder if anyone else ever took the time out to ask the question, WHY? Since no one has, I decided to go into my thoughts and into conversations I have had in the past to see why.

One of the main reasons it is so hard for a black man to be a man is because we do not know how. There is not a book or school. One of the most profound quotes that I have read said, "My dad did not teach me how to be a man; he lived and let me watch." Not making excuses but how many of us had someone to watch? The relationship a man has with his father is probably one of the most important relationships we can have for a few reasons. I will list a few. Reason one: We learn an innate trait that all men must have to survive. That trait should be a foundation for every man which is leadership. Every man needs to know how to lead, or we can say have balls, to put it in simpler terms. I have learned in the "few" relationships that I have been in that every woman wants to be led. Not in a chauvinistic way, but in a way that she is protected and has the confidence that she is going to be taken care of in any situation. Reason two: Confidence. As a child growing up, if you had your father in your life, there was nothing that you or your dad could not do. You can say that your father was or was supposed to be your first superhero. I have seen many black men lack the confidence needed in the world today to succeed and we replace it with this hard exterior of intimidation. The confidence that we learn and see as a child molds us to use that as we grow. Most men that I have talked to who were passive or very quiet in the relationship were either in a household with a domineering mother, no father, or had no male examples in their lives. They either watched their father sit back and do nothing while the mother ran the household. Some men had no father to get that confidence from, so it was never instilled. Young men were surrounded by women who showed the confidence that should have been shown by a man in the house. One of the most powerful things a black man, or any man, can do is to talk and look the individual in the eye that they are having a conversation. Eye contact says more than any words can ever say. That one small gesture is missing from so many men today. Reason three: if our fathers do not show us how to be men, we will learn on our own the wrong way, or someone else, influential or not, will show us. One of the things that is an unfair advantage to black men is that we must learn how to be a man on the fly. When most men are coming into manhood at the age of 18, black men are just coming to the realization that it is time to grow up. Where do we get the example of what it means to grow up? I would say not until the age of 25 to 27 that I realized okay I am now a man. I had made several mistakes with women, finances, career, and friendships. Some mistakes could have been avoided if I had the positive relationship that I needed with my father. This is one reason that we are behind the power curve because we take responsibility so late in life, when everyone else has taken that responsibility at an early age. The next part of this is that a man will learn how to be a man from the closet man around. Whether they are Strong or feminine, heterosexual or homosexual, businessmen or thugs, young men learn traits from the people that are closest to them. I strongly believe we have an innate moral compass of what is right and what is wrong. However, if there is no one to tell you how to handle situations, you grow up harnessing bad traits. Even if they are practiced long enough, they become the right traits or actions in our minds. So, the first relationship that is vital to establishing a healthy marriage is the relationship we have with our fathers. This relationship sets the foundation of how we run our households and many marriages fail because we overlook that we have a foundation that was never on stable ground. It is a foundation that is sure to fail unless you know how to cultivate the soil.

There was no doubt in my mind that one day, being a husband would be inevitable. It all started with a joke during Valentine's Day. It was another lonely day before the love holiday and I had no one to love. Not only did I not have anyone to love, but my vehicle was also in the shop. To get to work that day I asked one of my friends for a ride to work. She lived down the street from where I lived, and we worked in the same building. We started to talk; I asked what she was doing for Valentine's Day. She informed me that she would be going out with her boyfriend later, but for lunch, she would be spending it out with her female co-worker. "Me joking," I said, ask her if I could take her out for Valentine's Day. We laughed and there was not another thought about going on a date with her co-worker. Later that evening, my friend came down to my office and said CJ, my co-worker, will go out with you. I panicked. "What! You know I do not have a car," I said. She laughed and said you better figure it out. She gave me her number and walked back up to her office. This was on a Friday and my car would not be finished until Saturday, so the date would not go through. Instead of calling, I did nothing. There was no call, and for some reason, it felt like being quiet and out of sight was the right thing to do. A few days went by, maybe a week. My car was out of the shop, but my friend's co-worker was still on my mind. The weekend was approaching, and my friend's boyfriend played semi-pro basketball. The Old School Crew, as we called ourselves, had planned on going to the game. Knowing her co-worker would be there, I could not face her after standing her up without a call. I called my friend. What CJ is what she said because she knew this call was something different. "Can you call your co-worker and ask her if it's okay if I call her?" I asked.

She said, "You stood my girl up. Why does she want to talk with you?"

"Come on now, I am trying to make this right," I begged. A few minutes later, she called back, giving me the okay to make the phone call. It was a great phone call. We spoke for 7 hours straight. It started at 4:00 pm and we talked and laughed until 11:00 pm.

The next day, we met at the game, and we were inseparable from that point until we were not. Our first date was one for the ages. There I was a broke staff sergeant in the Air Force going on my first real date. In my pocket was one hundred and twenty dollars. It was all planned out. Twenty dollars for gas, fifty dollars apiece for dinner and if there was any change, it would be the tip. That was the plan. We got to the table at the Oyster Bar, and I browsed the menu and was not intimidated at all. This may be the night that someone I care about may become my lady. The waitress shows up and she orders her food. It's Lobster! On the inside, my throat dropped to the bottom of my stomach. She smiled and I smiled as if that was no problem. Then I knew there was a possibility that if running out of gas was an issue, then this could mean trouble for me. That night, we decided to become exclusive. The date was perfect, and we started dating.

Months later, things were going so well, but as everyone knows, deployment time was around the corner. It was my turn to deploy for 6 months. So many things began to go through my mind. There was a strong commitment. We had met each other's family. That was a first, bringing a woman home while in the military to meet my family. There was commitment between the two of us and somehow, we knew that this was not the end. While deployed, we talked whenever we could or until the operator disconnected our calls. We even discussed marriage while I was deployed and my commitment to her couldn't have been higher.

A lot of people, when they hear the word commitment, think of being committed to the other person and that is as far as it goes. I strongly believe that the reason that a lot of marriages do not work is because it is easier to get a divorce than to stay committed to making it work. In marriage, we are not only committed to the other person, but we need to also be committed to the relationship of marriage. Going into marriage I do not think we realize that it is not going to always be easy. Marriage is hard, then we bring in the other person's baggage, change, friends, and then their families. Let's explore a few of these. First, let's talk about baggage. When I say baggage, I am talking about our past hurts, our past failures, and our past disappointments. A lot of times, as men, it is hard for us to be vulnerable. I believe a lot of times, a man will not do right in relationships until he loses someone he loves. As men, we are conditioned to believe that the more women we have, the more man that it makes us. With this thought, we lie, cheat, and steal from women to get what we want, ultimately sex. Once we get sex, we conquer and move on. Once we find love and we are "committed," and the tables turn, not until then do we sympathize with the women in our life's past or present that we have hurt. At this point, we want to become serious and get into a relationship, but at the same time, we are going to bring that baggage of hurt from our past relationship. A man can get hurt one time and blame every woman from that point on to the future. Even though we go into marriage feeling loved in the back of our mind we still believe that you are going to do us the same way that the last woman did me. Not being cognoscente of all the women that we have hurt in our lives. In our relationships, the women take the brunt of the hurt that we felt from that one woman, which may be the root of why we do not trust, why we think you are going to leave, or why we do not believe that you love us as much as you say you do. It is hard to imagine that you are committed to us because you, even though you are not the one, have hurt us before. When we get into this situation, we do not know how to get out. The way to do that would be counseling and we know that is not going to happen, but we will visit that later. Men, we must realize that we bring a lot of baggage into the relationship that has not been dealt with. One thing that we must realize is that we have issues, we have hurts, and we have insecurities that need to be dealt with daily. The next thing that affects commitments in our marriage is change. If we were just aware that whom we are dating is not going to be the same one we marry, marriages would be so much easier. While you date, you see the best of both individuals, but what we do not understand as men is that this is not the same person that I am going to marry and when that happens, we do not know how to handle it. One thing that we hate as men is change. When we must deal with our wife changing in marriage, we think that we have been tricked. Once we feel that way, it is a man's duty to inform every man that we know not to get married

24

because the woman is going to change as soon as you say, "I do." We do not realize that what we did to fall in love and to make her fall in love, we must continue to do in marriage. A lot of times, we think that it is the wife that has changed, whether it's sexually, attitude, emotionally, or even that friendship that you have realized has dwindled since the marriage began. We do not realize that we have stopped opening the door; we do not realize that we have stopped giving out compliments; we do not realize that we have stopped meeting her at the door and finally, we do not realize that we have stopped dating. Once marriage begins, dating does not end. We automatically assume that she has changed, not that we have stopped doing the little things that we used to do when we dated. I have found that one of the biggest flaws in this instance is that your wife never says anything. For the ladies, if your man stops doing what you like, please let him know. If you do not, let him know and then it builds, when you do, tell him it is going to be considered nagging. No man likes a nagging woman! Women whether you think this is the situation or not, this is how we as men see it. The biggest change in marriage that we must realize is that we are the ones that change the most in marriage. The things that we stop doing cause the ones that we love to change, but we do not realize that because we are men, and we never change! That is something that we do not do. One of the hardest things about being married, I find, is trying to remember everything that she likes or dislikes. I have asked myself how this happened. I realized that the things that I used to do I do not do anymore. I had not done those things in so long that I had forgotten what she liked, what she did not like, or what was her favorite song or color. This is something we cannot do and must continue to work on.

Something that everyone seems to forget is how important the involvement of friends and family in the relationship is to a successful marriage. One thing I try to keep in my marriage is to keep my marriage between my wife and I and not between our friends and families. One mistake we make as men dealing with friends and families is telling too much of our business. I have a secret to let everyone know—men gossip just as much as women. We may be even worse. Sometimes, the least helpful information that we may receive may come from family and friends. We do not realize that when we ask for help from family and friends, they have only one interest in hand. That interest is ours. Our friends have our best interest in hand, and they may not be giving the best information that is good for the relationship. I have a saying in one of my CJisms that if you have a friend who has never told you you were wrong, they may not be your friends. We need to surround ourselves with friends and family who will tell us when we are right and when we are wrong. We do not need people around us who always tell us what we want to hear. Our friends should have our best interest at hand and sometimes that means telling us that we are wrong. What you relay to your friends about your wife builds the impression of what kind of wife you have. They do not know her, they only know what you tell them, so if everything you say is bad, then the impression that you have given your friends and family of your wife is bad. Regardless of how good your wife is, that is what friends and family are going to see. The acceptance of your wife may be a long time coming and very uncomfortable for her when there are gatherings to go out. We must remember that to our families and friends, our wives need to be our wives and if we know we do not have honest friends or family members to give us an unbiased opinion, we need to continue to praise and uplift our wives. We need to remember the view that our friends and families have of our wives is shaped by the things that have come out of our mouths about our wives. All these things play into our commitment. If we sit back and look at our situation, we must look and see whom we are really committed to in our relationship. Are we committed to the marriage, committed to the change, or committed to friends and family? These are questions that we need to ask ourselves.

During the deployment, we missed each other a lot and the topic of marriage was brought to the table. I was asked if I would marry her if the opportunity presented itself or do I thought she would be a good wife. I told her I knew she would be my wife from the time she ordered that lobster at The Oyster Bar, and I didn't say anything. We both laughed. The conversation never went any further than that, but in my mind, I had always seen her as my wife. The one thing about men is that we know what we want. We know if a woman can be someone that they are willing to marry or if they will just be a friend. I knew I wanted to marry her. Even though we are not together, there has never been one regret in asking for her hand in marriage. While deployed, I set the table. The ring was designed, the diamond was purchased, and the complete set was ready to be given. A few weeks after deployment, the question, "Will you Marry Me?" was about to be asked.

Now it was the time to figure out how would this be done. I go to the florist. Her favorite flower is the Cali Lilly. Those were way too expensive and at the time, they were out of season. My decision was to purchase four vases of different color flowers and put them throughout the house. Each flower would have directions. The first flower was as you walked into the house to the kitchen. The kitchen was the first place she always went because she put her lunch bag down. The note said to look at the kitchen table. There sat another flower that said go to the living room. The third flower said I would meet you in the bedroom. Once she arrived in the bedroom, there was the last flower and beside it on a crystal tree (she loved crystal), was the ring carefully tied hanging from the branch. I took the ring from the tree and got down on one knee and was ready to propose. She stopped me. She said wait, let's not do it here. Let's do it in the living room. I do not want to get proposed to in the bedroom.

This may have been one of the biggest missed red flags in any relationship that I have ever been a part of. On one of the supposedly happiest days of a woman's life, the location of the event overshadowed the actual event that was happening. This did not even come to mind the day I proposed. In my mind, it was if this is what she wants, let's go to the living room. After many years of self-reflecting, it made me realize that there are a lot of women who are living to have the life that they scripted versus the life that they are given. It also let me know that some women like to control every event in their lives, and it is nearly impossible to lead some women because they must control every aspect of the situation. Any situation, whether you or someone else, created the situation. Many women have had to be mother, father, and even counselor to so many people. In life, they had to rely on themselves to survive. This is all they know is how to control the situation to the best of their abilities. Because of this need to control, a lot of women have self-sabotaged their own relationships or the relationships their children have with their father. There are many men who do not like confrontation when it comes to women. Some of us say choose your battles wisely. I think this is one of our biggest mistakes is avoiding confrontation when it comes to our wives or significant others in relationships. This is not to say that we need to show them who is in control. However, it is to help us learn how to communicate during difficult situations. We have learned to bottle up our emotions for the sake of a happy wife, happy life mentality. This can and will be detrimental to the relationship. If it does not destroy it in the beginning, it will destroy the relationship in the end if it is not fixed or corrected on some level.

The planning of the wedding was next. We set the date for a year and a half later. In the excitement of being excited, we decided to push the date up to February 7, 2005. In hindsight, February 7 would be the day of reckoning in many aspects of my life. Her dad asked why are you moving the date up? Is there any difference that getting married then versus waiting to marry in a year and a half? I think he figured that she was pregnant, and we wanted to make it right in the eyes of the Lord. There were many things we wanted to make right in the eyes of the Lord, but pregnancy was not on the horizon. It would not be in the future, either. Before getting married, we decided there would be no more sex before marriage. We would be struggling with going to church together and then coming back to her place and having sex on a makeshift pallet on the floor. We would make it through every week and then on Sunday after church, we get our Sunday "Nap" in and make love on the makeshift pallet. Her conviction is what drove the guilt and the waiting for the next week to be right back in the same position. I wanted to make it work; however, my discipline was poor in those situations because I went from a man who could get sex anytime he wanted to a man who loved his fiancé and would do anything to marry this woman. Pushing the wedding date up helped her and me out in this situation. The waiting until marriage did not work either, but we did agree not to move in together until we were married. That was something we agreed on. I would recommend that if you are getting married, get a place together because your place will always be your place and her place will always be her place. Not until you both get things together will you be able to claim those things as husband and wife.

The big day had arrived. I must say it was the happiest day of my life. Finally, there was someone who loved me unconditionally. There was never a doubt in my mind that she loved me. Today, I still do not doubt that she loved me. It was the day before we had the wedding rehearsal and things were complete. I went to my home one last time. There was not a bachelor party, and my boys were very disappointed at that, however, for the first time in a long time, I was content with the woman I was about to marry and did not need a bachelor party. Prior to this night, the women and stories were to give me the acceptance that I was yearning for to prove that I was a man. In this moment before my wedding, it made me feel complete. There was no going to sleep, no regrets, and I would be marrying the woman of my dreams.

The day had arrived. In a room with my groomsmen and waiting to see her walk down the aisle, I knew she would be gorgeous; her style was impeccable, and she raved about her gown even though she would not give me a hint of how it looked or how much it cost. Before the wedding started, I went to her dressing room and gave her a bridal gift. It was a gold necklace with a diamond cross. It went perfectly with her gown. She reached through the door and gave me my gift. It was engraved cuff links with CJ on the links. They were perfect. Quickly, I went back to the room to put on the cuff links. It was showtime.

After everyone arrived, down the aisle was my future wife. Coming through the speakers was Darian Keith Horn, With This Ring. This song was picked by me, and I still listen to the song because I truly believe God chose her to be an answer to all my prayers. Thanks to the pastor tapping me on the shoulder, I was getting ready to lose it. She was everything that I hoped and prayed for. She was the most beautiful bride I had ever seen.

The wedding, in many aspects was a blur. There were highlights that were remembered, but being married was all that mattered to me. The people that I wanted there were there, the people I loved were there and it was a moment that will never be forgotten. However, there was a little disappointment that a couple of my brothers were not there. My brothers mean a lot to me. They may not know, but I am the combination of all my brothers. Watching them made a tremendous impact on my life. Because they were not all there, it caused me to change my speech for the wedding. It still was one of my life's favorite moments.

After the lights were turned off, all the cameras were gone, and we were alone in the hotel, reality set in for us both. We were married. We were both married but nearly too tired to consummate the marriage. As we laughed there was a sense of calmness that came over me. A calmness that said that my life was complete. Not being able to tell what she felt, however, I did not feel that she regretted our decision. The next morning, we woke up to start this new journey, both of us energized and, at the same time, not looking towards her pending deployment that we be a week after our marriage. One thing about the military is that if you are married, you will be tested. It will test your faith, it will test your commitment, it will test your trust, and it will test your decisions. Out of seven years of marriage, we were tested. Tested to the point where we went an entire year and only saw each other for three days in the year. My strong belief is that no one gets married with the intent of getting divorced. Never did I think divorce would be an option in my marriage. How could it be? Our biggest arguments came from me putting pillows on the couch, wiping the mirror after brushing my teeth, oh and me buying an eight-hundred-dollar camera. Well, I did tell her I was going to the store and get a camera. She didn't ask how much it cost. It was a lesson learned. She never forgot to ask me how much anything cost again.

To me, my marriage was good, it was fulfilling so I thought. It was not until the two years that we lived in Turkey that I started to see that marriage will always require work. My wife was talented. She was a godly woman, could sing, she was smart, she danced, and she was one of the most beautiful women that I have seen to this day. However, having all those things does not save a marriage if you do not put in the work. Turkey was a test for us. We were forced to make some hard decisions. Our marriage had been going on now for about five years. This was in between deployments due to military commitments. For a while I had been feeling that we were not having enough time for ourselves. She oversaw the praise dance team and I played basketball nearly every day was a normal day in Turkey. We talked; well, I stopped talking because not saying anything was my way of communicating. Now, it is known that this is not the best way to communicate, it was my go-to when something was happening in the house that I did not like. She realized that we were not spending enough time and every night for about three days in a row, she would come home, shower, put on a nice negligée and we would enjoy each other's company. There was never any conversation because we both were tired. On the fourth day this happened, things changed. I sat on the couch and watched television as if I did not notice the nice red negligee that she had on. Probably one of the toughest tests and most stubborn situations that I have ever been in. In my mind, it was my way of communicating that it was not about sex. It was the time that was needed by me to spend with my wife. At that moment, two things happened. One was the flashback of me being alone and feeling empty because sex was never an issue. I wanted my wife. It was not about sex. It was the enjoyment of my wife. Secondly was the hurt that was felt by my wife that inside, it was a decision that I made that I could never recover from because of the way I made her feel.

There is nothing wrong with being selfish. The problem that comes from being selfish happens when the individual in question does not know that they were selfish. We were both selfish in our moments. However, as a man in marriage, I have learned that I am the gatekeeper of my home. I am expected to lead, provide, and appreciate my wife. If these things are done, my wife will nurture me and take care of my needs. So many times, as men, we look at what the woman's responsibilities are in the marriage and forget about the responsibilities we have as men. I was one of those men. Even though cooking is one of my favorite pastimes, sometimes wanting to see my wife cook for me was something I wanted. It is not that she would not do it, she knew cooking was my thing, so why bother? In a marriage, one of my beliefs is that if you give a man consistent sex and peace, you will not have to worry about the man going outside of the house. Another one of my beliefs was my wife could read my mind and if I wasn't speaking, you have this woman superpower that says, "His problem is 1, 2, or 3." The biggest breakdown in my marriage was communication. As men, we say women nag or want to argue all the time. The saying is true: the squeaky wheel gets the oil. This leads to us making sure she is satisfied so we do not have to hear her mouth. A Happy Wife and a Happy Life must be one of the most detrimental saying to a marriage. This is because if this is happening nine times out of ten, the husband is not being heard. Even with these beliefs, the core of the dysfunction is selfishness. This does not come from the woman, but it comes from the man. She was taken care of because her husband didn't want to hear her complain. She was ignored not because she neglected her husband but because her husband did not know how to communicate. She did not provide consistent sex because her husband wanted it when he wanted it, but he did not make her feel wanted. We, as men, say that most of these issues of today that is the reason women are not married. However, these are just reactions that we reciprocate from being selfish men.

We never really recovered from that situation; however, we were able to still have happy times in our marriage. The thing about my wife and I was we loved to shop. Shop therapy always eased the pain or helped communication on any level. The other thing that helped was we were leaving Turkey to be stationed in Minot, ND. We joked that we would be the only black couple in Minot when we arrived. It was by far the most miserable news that we could get. My functional manager informed me that the reason it was ND was because my wife was in a critical career field and that is where we both had to go. There was no getting out of this one assignment. Two things crossed my mind. One, I knew this would be my last assignment because I only ever wanted to do twenty years in the military and there were only two years and a few months left before my retirement. Second, this was my wife and if it meant North Dakota, then North Dakota was it. From the time we stepped on Minot AFB, she was plotting ways to get out of North Dakota. North Dakota was weird. I can not pinpoint what caused a rift between us, but it was the same story. Change bases and then deploy. Duty had called for me to go to Iraq for six months and two months after my deployment, she was hit with a notice to be leaving also. At my fifth month of a six-month deployment, she would deploy. We had arranged that we could meet in Iraq for three days before she was off to her deployment site in Iraq. In my heart of hearts this is where it is believed by me that my marriage was lost. This was a rough deployment for her. There were times she would call me crying because of the constant bombing. She would tell me that she had been days without showers and that she did not know what day it was. Knowing my wife, she was still an airman and got the job done. That was just her. She was always Superwoman.

Life after that was so different when she returned. It was stressful in the house. As an airman, one of my biggest struggles throughout the Air Force was managing or passing my fitness assessment. For years, this had been an issue. So much of an issue that I was reported years prior to the base Command Chief for disciplinary actions. It did not work because the Command Chief was like, "It is obvious something is wrong with the system or his taping because he looks great in his uniform." He had me come into his office to tell me that he was not going to give me any discipline and to keep working out. The elephant in the room had returned and upon my wife's return, I was dealing with the same weight issue. I met the requirements on my run, push-ups, and sit-ups but failed miserably on my taping. It had made it to the point where I was to see the Command Chief again at a different base. Even though we were both home, it seemed as mentally this was a process that I navigated alone. Leaving Minot, ND, was still my wife's priority. She had finally received notification that she was selected for a job at the Pentagon. She was leaving in ninety days. She asked what I thought about her relocation. She said that it was possible for me to get orders also, but I would need to reenlist. That was out of the question twenty years was always my goal. Reenlisting or extending an assignment to leave earlier was not going to happen. It was not going to happen with the pending decision looming on my fitness assessment failures. It was one thing she asked before she was to leave. Let's make sure our household is together. This may have been one of the biggest façades that I have ever been a part of in life. We played it well for the cameras, but the cracks were inevitable after the flash was out of your eyes.

The relationship of marriage will be one of the hardest things that we do as men, but one of the main things we must change about marriage is our attitudes. There is a notion that marriage is like the beginning of the end, does not encourage us to support the institution of marriage. A lot of people will not get married because they have not heard or seen any good stories about marriage. As men, we need to promote marriage because whether we want to believe it or not, we are better married than single. Whether we want to believe it or not, we are in a struggle every day. No one will understand what we go through as black men better than our wives. Or should I say no one should understand our struggle more than our wives? I say this because, as men, we have this notion that we are to be tough and keep the façade we can take on the world. I have a saying, yes, another one that I have broad shoulders; I can carry what you bring on. In reality, no one can carry the weight of the world, no matter how much we try. One of the highlights I enjoy about marriage is when I get home, I can let my guard down. I could tell her how I feel or how I have been wronged. I think, as a black man, only a few people can understand going into a store and getting followed because of the color of your skin. When I get home, I want to be able to share my feelings and have someone there who can understand my struggle. That should be your wife. The bond between you and your wife should be filled with strength and vulnerabilities. When

40

you walk out your door, you should be able to take on the world for those eight to sixteen hours, but when you come home, it is your wife who is there to say I am proud of you. You do not have to be strong for me at home because I know what kind of man you are, and I am proud of you for being what I need. That is what we need to hear as men.

After she arrived in Washington, DC, we agreed that she would stay with her uncle until my retirement was complete. My time in the military would be up in February and it was now July. We agreed that we would see each other every three months. Our first visit was in October and we met in Minneapolis, MN. The first night was great; however, something was not right. We were close but distant and it seemed after three months, we would be happy to see each other, but for some reason, there was distance. This visit was not a good visit, and it would be the last visit that we would have since our departure from our well-put-together marriage, so it seemed. We left and went in opposite directions. She headed to DC. I headed back to Minot for a few more months until retirement. As I drove back to Minot, there was still the decision as to what would happen with me and my fitness assessment evaluation. Not once did we speak about it and in my mind, I had made it up that I was a disappointment to my wife. What would we do? At the time, my bachelor's degree was not completed and obtaining a master's was the furthest thing from my mind. Now, there was a possibility of getting kicked out with four months left to hit twenty years. Deep down, I believed it was an issue because we had conversations about it. She came home from work and was so frustrated that she said people frustrated her and as I inquired with what people, she said uneducated people. My response was, "I am uneducated. What are you saying?"

"You are different," she said. However, I did not let it go. In my opinion, you may need a break from your job.

"Just because someone does not have an education, it does not mean that they can or cannot do the job," I said. She agreed. We chalked it up as frustration, but in the back of my mind, it was always a thought as to if she thought that of her husband. So much was happening and the way we departed added to the stress that was already there. It was depression at its best. At work, Sgt Jones was still handling business, while at home you could hardly walk in the house because of junk and clutter. Sleep and more sleep were the only things that mattered to me.

A month had passed, and we had good days and we had bad days. We were back and I wanted to see her so bad I lied to her. This one small lie led to the destruction of our marriage. The desire to see her had me miss bill payments to save for a plane ticket back to Minneapolis.

Not wanting her to know that a ticket was purchased, I called and told her that a friend of mine had given me a ticket to use to meet in Minneapolis. It was free, I told her, not knowing the cost would be unobtainable. At first, she was happy then it was a quietness. We spoke some more, and we hung up the phone. About 20 minutes later, she called back. She said CJ, I do not want to come. "Why? Do you have something to do?" I exclaimed.

"No!" she said, trying to convince her did not happen and we hung the phone up after an argument. She insisted that she did not want to go and was upset that it was hard for me to understand. To me, it did not make sense. She said she was not coming, that was it and we both hung up the phone. This is a trip for me to see my wife and a ticket for you to see your husband. After sitting there in disbelief, my mind began to race. Go look at the bank account, go look at the phone bill. There must be a reason she does not want to come.

While checking the bank account, I saw purchased tickets for the Cherry Blossom Festival. Bingo, that was it. Not only was there one ticket purchased but there were two tickets purchased. Immediately, I called back and before hello could be spoken, I said, "Who was going with you because you purchased two tickets?" She calmly said the second ticket was for our friend who introduced us. They both were in DC during this time. Okay was my only answer as I hung up and remained mad because, on one hand my fears were cooled because it wasn't someone else and two there still was a plane ticket that could not be used, and bills were not paid.

She said that it was the Cherry Blossom Festival and she wanted to go to the festival. "Does the festival happen every year?" I asked. She told me the Cherry Blossom Festival happened every year. My thoughts were to skip it this year; we will be together next year, and we could attend together. She still refused to meet in Minneapolis.

Two days had passed, and we had not spoken with each other. To me, this was sort of normal after an argument. Then suddenly, the phone rang, it was my wife. With enthusiasm, I said, "Hey babe."

She said hello, but it wasn't a good hello. Her next words were, "I don't want to do this anymore."

"Do what? What do you mean?" I said. Divorce was the furthest thing from my mind. She said she did not want to be in the marriage anymore. *Over a plane ticket,* I thought. For the next couple of months, it probably was the worst part of my life. Most time was spent telling my wife that divorce is not needed. She didn't want to listen. She was done. My last-ditch effort was to call her mom. As I called, I was asked if she could speak with her daughter to tell her let's work it out and not divorce. She told me you asked my daughter for a divorce. "Never did I do that," I said. If that was the case, this call would not have been made for you to speak with her.

She seemed surprised and she said, "Well, that is between you and my daughter."

Defeated! I said, "I understand. Thank you, ma'am." I hung up the phone. The reality set in that divorce was inevitable.

No one gets married to get divorced. Divorce is an emotional roller coaster that takes you in directions that you never thought you would go. The stages of divorce for me were very dark and scary. Alone in ND with no one really understanding what I was going through. The only thing that kept me from thinking about ending it all was a promise I heard from God at an early age. He said, "You were not put here to fail." In all situations, I am reminded of this. Those words have allowed me to continue regardless of any situation in my life. You were not put here to fail. With my career and my marriage in the balance, my only saving grace was a co-worker who is a dear friend to me today. She said do not be walking around here like you have it all together. She was going through a divorce also and she was like this shit is hard. She was there when a conversation needed to be had. She was there when someone was needed to listen and help me process things. We even coached a youth center basketball team together and the kids and her saved my life. No matter what was needed, she was there. Even during her deployment, she would call back to check on me. We both joked that we were not doing this marriage shit again. We both ended up engaged again. The irony of both of our situations. Finally, it was decision time on my career and punishment for failing my fitness assessments.

On day, I went to meet with the group commander. He asked what should happen. After explaining that people must be measuring me wrong and that I look presentable in my uniform, I asked one thing. "Sir, throughout my career, I have been a great leader, worker, and non-commissioned officer. It is understandable to meet the standard and maintain the standard. If you look at my test, I have maxed out my sit-ups and maxed out my push-ups. My run time for the mile and a half is between fourteen and fifteen minutes. I am at the gym every morning (He knew because he would see me there). I have one month in the military to reach twenty years. My wife has relocated to the Pentagon and is requesting a divorce. The only thing that I ask is to let me retire in front of my airmen," I asked. The room was silent. He said Sergeant Jones, you may leave. After leaving the room, my stomach turned in knots. My thought was you just stood in the room full of white men and pleaded for your career. At that moment, I vowed this was a situation that I would never put myself in again. After making a few calls to see what the worst is and what the best could happen in this situation. I was content. Two days later, the wing commander had me on the calendar for my fate appointment. We walked into the wing commander's office. The irony of this situation was the wing commander was bigger than me. For him to even pass a fitness assessment they would have to tape him at his chest, and he would still have to run a mile and a half in under ten minutes. It was impossible for him to pass. However, the tough lesson was when the rabbit has the gun, it does not matter what you think should happen. You must play by the rabbit rules. He looked at my records and asked a few questions and I answered. He asked if there was anything that needed to be said and I declined. In my mind, I had accepted the worst punishment. I knew I would retire and get a pension for the rest of my life and that whatever happened would not be a detriment to my retirement pay. In my mind, the military had taken everything from me, my family, my wife, and my dignity. What more could you do to me? Give me my punishment and let me get back to figuring out this divorce and life thing. The punishment was in, a few weeks before my retirement date, a stripe was taken away. It was over, in my mind, they had won. They succeeded in humiliating me and making an example out of an arrogant black man who felt like he was untouchable. It was personal to me again and it would not go unnoticed.

However, my marriage was my priority. We discussed how we would divide everything and where I would go. We had discussed that we would put the divorce off until I left Minot and try to work on it for a year before we filed. We agreed and that had settled my mind. Three days later, divorce paperwork was received in the mail. Devastated again, I called and asked why, and she said it was not needed to wait. We went back and forth and finally, I said, "If I sign these papers, I am done. Do you want me to sign these papers?"

She said, "Yes!" There was a divorce lawyer downtown Minot that I visited to review the papers.

He asked, "Did she had these written up?"

"Yes, she did. Why do you ask?" I said.

He said, "She is taking all the bills except your car payment and phone bill, and neither one of you can touch your retirement or savings plan."

I told him, "I had not read the divorce papers. He was the first to read them. Just tell me where to sign. This is not something that I agree with doing." He asked me to come back and get the papers in two to three days and we could sign them at that moment. The big day had come—It was February 7, 2012. This was the day for me to officially leave the military and head back to the East Coast. It was bittersweet. As I left Minot, I vowed never to cross the Mississippi River ever again.

As I went down the interstate listening to the radio, through the speaker came Marvin Sapp, "So glad I made it. I made it through in spite of the storm and rain, Heartache, and pain, still alive, declaring I made it through. See, I didn't lose; I experienced loss at a major cost, But I never lost faith in you." By the time the verse was over, on the side of the road, I was parked crying because I still believed His promise as a young boy. You were not put here to fail. I prayed and thanked God. After getting myself together there was a calmness that came over me. It was time to stop by the lawyer's office to pick up the divorce papers. As I enter, he is waiting for me and asks if I am ready. Ready as I am going to get, so I sign the papers. He goes to sign the papers then he stops. He says, "Do you know what's today?"

I said, "My retirement."

He said, "No, today is your anniversary." Seven years to the exact date I was getting divorced. On this date, February 7, for me had been my marriage, my retirement, and my divorce. What a day, he signed and said he would put the papers in the mail. I left to head back east. Not

49

knowing what to expect of my new life was not scary now. I was still excited. I knew I was not put here to fail. There was a new energy. Still yearning for my wife but understanding the situation I had finished. It wasn't a win, but I finished! The first to finish in some situations, but it didn't feel like a win, but I was content. *I finished!*

CJ-ism #22 - *Not until men stop seeing showing emotions as a sign of weakness, will we ever be able to love our women the way they supposed to be loved!*

Chapter 2: The Mother, The Father, & Me

One thing to realize in relationships is that siblings have different relationships with their parents. All the feelings and views are not the same. As siblings, we have our ideas of how great or how bad our parents were or are to us. Most arguments are caused because some views of parents may be different and some siblings can't or will not realize even though you have the same parents, the relationship can be drastically different. The relationship that was between my parents and me was by far the most difficult relationship that is relevant in my life. My mother was a hardworking lady, about five foot five and had a heart of gold to many people. For most of my life, my mom worked as a housekeeper at local hotels and would work five days and sometimes six days a week. She didn't start working until it was time for me to start kindergarten. Prior to that, I remember her helping me spell my name, memorize my numbers and ABCs, and even tie my shoes before starting school. We always had fruit trees at our home. The first place we lived there was a cherry tree and in the backyard was a huge tree that housed honeybees. Sometimes, we would go out to the tree and pull out a honeycomb for honey or pick cherries from the cherry tree in the yard. Later, we would move to the family land where there was an apple orchard, pear tree, and plum trees. My mother was very smart. Even though she only had and eighth-grade education, she had knowledge of many things, but she would get frustrated when someone would not let her get her thoughts out or tell her that she was wrong. Many times, my actions have mirrored her behavior as well. Many people loved my mom, and she loved many people. If she didn't care for you, you could tell it on her face. She did not hide it very well.

My dad was sort of tall and very kind. This sometimes caused people to try to take advantage of him. However, he was aware. Because my dad could not read or write, many thought he didn't know what he was talking about. To survive and be productive in the world as dad, there had to be a level of smartness even though the education did not match. One trait I know I received from my dad is that he was prideful. It's not only a trait in my dad but a trait in all my dad's brothers as well. There was no way that it could not have been passed down as a well-received Jones trait. Drinking and smoking were a staple in my dad's life at an early age. It was the norm, but outside of the drinking, Dad was very funny. His sense of humor was something to love and cherish. No matter what was going on, he was quick with a joke or a comeback. There were many years that I wanted to know more and more about my dad, but those talks were never discussed. Many people would tell me different stories about how great my dad was playing baseball. Not once did he ever mention that he played baseball. Not until recent years did I totally understand my dad. The understanding of why the feeling of him not being there, the feeling of not feeling a connection, and the reason for all the pride were made clear when my dad and I had a car ride that changed my view completely.

As children, we want to impress our parents. We long for our parents to say I love you or I am proud of you. Many times, we want to be like our parents. Things for me have been totally different. As stated earlier, a young boy will learn how to be a man by the example given by the closest man in his life. For me, that was my dad. In my heart, it feels as if I grew up without a dad. However, I had a chance to watch my dad. For the longest time, it was resentment and me spending most of my life trying to do the opposite of what my dad was doing. For a long time, there was a fear of me drinking to get drunk because of the fear of being like my dad. The school was always important to me because it was always known that my dad could not write or read, so it was a motivation to be better. Treating women with respect and having only one woman was very important to me because of the day of remembered my dad speaking of other women. This affected me so much that for a while, there were only female friends because if there was no commitment, then we were technically not in a relationship. Everything that was me was modeled on not being like my dad.

Fathers are so important to have healthy relationships. This is true for women and men. There are so many intricacies that come with being a man that it is nearly impossible for a woman to teach. To see my daughter without her mother is something that, as a father, wished to never happen. A daughter needing a mother and a son needing a father is irreplaceable. When mothers say they are the mother and the father, there is something that runs through my veins that says toxic. To think that, as a woman, you can replace what a child needs from a man is toxic. Also, for a man to say he is the mother and the father would be toxic. A mother and father, whether by birth, choice, or circumstance, are needed and there is no substitute. In my opinion, the destruction of the black family started with the drugs being infiltrated in our communities and the separation of mothers and fathers in relationships. The use of public assistance was a way to keep men out of the house. Assistance was withheld from families if the man was in the household. It is my belief that men should work. However, there is a strong belief by me that men do want to support their families. We are intricate individuals who need healing and many more things that have destroyed the black man.

One of my favorite books is called "Men Cry in the Dark." The book is a great read, but one of the reasons the book sticks out to me is because of the title. This was the first time that it was said to me directly or indirectly. There was always and still is today, a stigma that real men do not cry. It's less relevant today because more men are showing emotions, but the narrative of Real Men Don't Cry is real. My dad, in my eyes, was a giant. Not size-wise but because of his personality, his laugh, and his ability to survive. There was a resentment that made me have a feeling of missing out on a real father because my dad was there but not there. One of the realest conversations I had with my dad was a drive we had to my uncle's house. The affection between me and my dad was not there, but like my dad, words cut and are the most harmful to us. One day, we went to a family member's house and the family member continuously discounted everything my dad said. He was getting frustrated and once it was noticed, suggesting leaving was the right thing to do before things got out of control. While riding back, I asked, "Why did you get mad." He said, "Well, I am tired of people calling and thinking that I am stupid. Because I did not go to school and cannot read or write, they think that I do not know anything. I wanted to go to school, but Poppa had me out working so they could go to school. Now they treat me like I am dumb." As my dad started to cry, it seemed as if words had left me. The driving continued and as he continued to shed tears, I said, "It is fine, I still love you. It will be fine." At this moment, beside me, sat a man who was broken. A man who had lived on pride and looked for acceptance from the ones he loved the most. Beside me; Sat me! The man who wanted love from his family. The man who received love from everyone else except the ones that he wanted to accept love. My dad continued to speak, "I want you to know that I am proud of you. Don't ever let anyone tell you what you know or do not know. I love you." He then began to apologize for crying and I immediately stopped him because, at that moment, it explained everything that was disliked about my dad. It showed me a little boy who didn't have a childhood but lived to take care of his siblings so that they could have the childhood that he did not have. It showed me a survivor who survived through all odds with the only way of communicating was with his voice. A voice that spoke, but most times, he felt it was not heard. He was a man who had to live off trusting everyone he encountered because there was no way of verifying if they were telling the truth. A prideful man who had to put his pride aside every day and believe everyone that he had encountered was genuine. We drove a little further, and my dad cracked a joke. It broke the ice and we talked until we returned to my dad's house. Before leaving, he gave me a hug and for the first time my dad was understood, and forgiveness was granted to my dad by me. Driving away with the realization that my dad didn't know how to be a dad. He could not give me what was needed by me because he never received it. My dad could not be a father because he did not know how. It was like looking in a mirror, in the military, my life was a mirror of trying to be a husband, trying to lead individuals, and trying to be the best me with other people telling me that you were not trying. In my mind, my dad was a giant, but on that day, a giant was destroyed and witnessing it was devastating. It didn't take weapons. It only took words. Words destroy and it was words that fractured the relationship with my mom and me.

Growing up, being a teacher was my career goal. A math teacher at Franklinton High School and later that would transition to the mayor of the town. Those were my dreams and those are the things that were said from the ninth through the twelfth grade. Everyone knew that for sure; however, the message wasn't always loud and clear. After graduating high school, my studies continued attending college at St. Augustine's College, a private college in Raleigh, NC. It was not my first choice. However, it was a great experience until deciding to leave because me having my own money was more important at the time than having an education. Once leaving school, the United States Air Force would be my next stop. It was a quick process for enlisting. Within three months, my journey began by heading to San Antonio, TX, for basic training. This, by far was the biggest decision made upon leaving high school. My first choice was to join the US Army. My brother was in the Army and for some reason, the picture of him that hung on my mother's wall always intrigued me; however, the Air Force would be the final decision. When it comes to who molded me, it was my brothers. I tried my best to mimic and copy my brothers. Once the idea that the military was on my radar, there was an appointment with the Army recruiter. My mother quickly called my brother, and he came to speak with me. He informed me that if the military was something that I wanted to do, then the Air Force should be my first choice. On that day, we called the recruiter for the Army and cancelled the appointment. It was a decision that turned out to be great, however, some said the Army would be too hard for me to succeed. Hell, some said the military period would be too demanding to succeed. This was happening over the break from college, and it was time to return to school. The school was going great; my name was on the Dean's List. My college roommates were ecstatic for me. Three out of the 6 of us had made the Dean's List, but in the back of my mind was still the impending decision of going to the military. Getting back to school, there was still and urge that school was not quite the right fit. Teaching was always there, but going back to school and not having money was too much on my pride and ego. Even though throughout college there are many broke students. In my circle of friends, it was me. Of the six of us, two came from a well-off family, one was from Africa and had access to money, one was an aspiring singer and drug dealer who sang and sold drugs, and then the last roommate was just there in school to sell drugs. So, it bothered me even though, as it is reflected now, my pride to be like the crowd overrode, the real reason that my attending college was important. The final straw was asking my mother to let me have money to get clothes for school. Growing up, it was natural that on the first day of school, you had new clothes. It did not matter if it was three pairs of pants, four shirts, and a pair of shoes that were a staple in going to school. Things were different in college.

"Hey Ma!" I spoke. "Are you going to give me some money to buy clothes for school?" "You have clothes for school. Why do you need some more clothes?" she asked.

"Well, it is the first day of school and I need clothes to go back," I explained.

"You are already at school, so you do not need new clothes. You know that loan you took out to go to school, I will have to start paying that back. So, you may need to look for a job to pay that loan back. I do not have any money to give you to buy new clothes," she said. That was all that needed to be heard. The next day at lunch, my walk began into a new life, a new journey, and a new chapter of being independent. The mile-and-a-half walk to the recruiter station would start everything.

After checking out of school within a month, my first flight on a plane was a flight to San Antonio, Texas, to Lackland Air Force Base. It would be the first time on a flight and the first time in my life that fending for myself was the only option. During my time at basic training, contact with family members was limited. However, there was a lot of contact with my family when the beginning of technical school started. We were in Denver, Colorado, at Lowry Air Force Base. Freedom is what it was at that time, but missing my family can still be remembered. Missing my family was hard for me. There had never been a time that being away from my family lasted for more than a week or two weeks. Now, we had been apart for two months and only communicated with limited phone calls. Receiving letters from family was the highlight of everyone's day. One day, the receiving of a letter would alter the relationship between my mom and me forever.

There was excitement to open the letter because it was from my mom. My mom had not written me a letter since leaving for basic training, so excited for the letter, I opened the letter in class during lunch. It said, "Hello, how are you doing? I hope you are fine, and I hope that you are doing well. I am writing this letter to let you know that I am disappointed in you. You have left here, and you have forgotten all about your family. It is like you do not even love your family anymore. You have not sent any money back to help me with this college loan. You said you wanted to be a preacher when you grow up, and that is not the way any preacher should act." This is just the part of the letter that was remembered and to this day, not much more is remembered. We had a test in class that day and there is no remembrance of taking the test. I passed, but how is a mystery to me. Maybe the test was taken before the letter. The last part of the day was spent sending a reply to the letter that was received. It read, "I am sorry to disappoint you, but that was not my intent. Currently, I am in technical school, and we have not really started making any money for me to send back home. I love my family and how can you say I do not love my family because I did not send any money back home? All the time growing up, you all have been telling me I am going to be just like my daddy, and now you are saying I don't love my family because of money. It is obvious that you were not listening to me because I have never once said I wanted to be a preacher. I have always said I wanted to be a teacher. I am disappointed also." Just like reading the letter, writing the letter, this is the only part that can be remembered. However, both letters were three pages long and neither letter was showing I love you, but both ended with I love you.

The letter eventually could have been fixed. However, the next thing took mending the relationship or even thinking about paying the loan back a hard pill to swallow. The next couple of weeks, there were received letters from my sisters. Most of the letters said that an apology to my mother was owed. One of my sisters apologized. She said she apologized for saying that I would be just like my daddy. She said that she only wanted me to do better and that if I needed anything, to let her know. She understood why the letter took the tone that it took because of the feelings that were expressed in the letter. She even sent me her calling card number and told me to call her whenever it was needed. Today, apologies go out to her because that calling card was run up until it was turned off. Remember, I was in Colorado. However, her letter meant the world to me at that time because, in my mind, my mother had turned the family against me. Why would she let them read the letter? Did she tell them what she sent to me? Being a disappointment to my own mother hurt deeply. When did I ever say I wanted to be a preacher? These questions haunted me for a long time. We never spoke of the letter, but in my mind, this was the beginning of my relationship with my mother and its distant relationship. Even though it was understood by me that my mother was proud of me. Wanting to hear it was longed for in my life.

During my time in the military something that we looked forward to receiving calls from family. Whether it was five or ten minutes, those calls carried us until the next call. There were not many calls from my family, but when I returned home, there was a feeling that it was good to see you. My mom would want me to go over to everyone's house to see them. That is something that is normal when any military member goes home. She would make sure that there was a Sunday dinner before I left to return to base, and I would always leave with a hug or hug and kiss. For some reason this did not ever let me forget about the letter. To me, disappointing my mother always played in my head. The loan that she questioned was not paid back because, on the other end, Fannie Mae was getting college loan payments from me also. So as an up-and-coming Airman, my funds were low also. During this time, my mom stopped working. It was told to me that my mom stopped working because the Internal Revenue Service had started to garnish her taxes and she was not working to give the government her money. To me, that was devastating because the son that she said was a disappointment was continuing to disappoint.

One of the first relationships a child has is the relationship they have with their parent. The most important thing not to do is to disappoint your parents. My daughter is my everything and even though, because of the circumstances, we do not see each other physically every day, one thing she hates to do is disappoint her daddy. Once, I told my daughter that she disappointed daddy and she cried like she had never cried before. It was the tears, the snot, and the hyperventilating and all. After calming her down and thinking about it, that instance took me back to how I felt when my mom told me that she was disappointed in me. When a child knows that they have been disappointed they will do whatever it is in their power to try to fix it. The ironic part is that most of the time, you do not know how because proper communication has not been given after the disappointment. You only know what not to do to get in that particular situation again, but you do not communicate with each other to see if the actions have really solved the disappointment. As a child, whether young or adult, you go by blindly trying to receive approval for something that you do not know the ask. This leads to the child thinking that you can never do enough to satisfy the parent.

As my career continued to grow in the military, there were many awards that were received. Many thoughts came to mind trying to make my mom proud. What could be given to my mom to make her proud? Something that can be displayed and eventually something that she could say that she was proud of me. In my mind, that would clear my doubt of disappointing her. Never did I think that my mother did not love me. That would be impossible, she birthed me. Not liking me was another question. In my opinion, was I my mother's favorite? No!

Did my mother love me? Yes! Did my mother like me? Maybe? For some reason, there was not a feeling of like coming from my mom. It was nothing she ever did or said to make that a fact, but there were things that were picked up on. Could these things have been because my pinpointing every negative thing that was said was now the normal behavior for me? Did disappointing my mother make me key in on all the negative that was said or perceived because wanting to fix it was something in the back of my mind that needed to be fixed? Regardless of what it was, the relationship with my mom never seemed to get on track between us and it affected me by the woman that was chosen to date and marry. There were many times that my mom gave me the impression that she was selfish and in most of my relationships, women, in my opinion, was selfish. It was coming true that you would date someone like your mother or you would date someone like your father if you were a woman. What was learned was you will date someone who will give you the same issues as you had with your parents unless you fix the issue. That requires communication with your parents about your feelings and being brave enough to say how you feel about a situation without feeling that you are disappointing your parents. Also, as a parent, this requires listening! My parents were my parents and if there was a chance to do a do-over, there is not much that would be changed. The man who sits here today is because of my parents. The flaws and all, they are the reason. However, they have given me a newfound respect for what it takes to be a parent. My mother and father have passed and one of the loneliest feelings in the world is to know that you are in this world without a mother or a father.

At the end of the day, there was love by my parents. There is a belief by me that my mother loved me, but she did not like me. There is also a belief by me that my dad thinks that my success was far more than he expected. Now that the opportunity of being a parent has been given to me, it is understood. It is understood that there is no playbook in parenting. It is understood that your abilities only go as far as your experiences. After that you are looking and asking for the right answers. It is understood that as a parent, you are expected to know everything without the question being asked if you know or if you need help. It is understood that parenting is hard and demanding. Understanding that every day is not going to be your best, but giving your best on that day is a requirement. Finally, understand as a parent that regardless of what you do, the critic in this situation is your child and you can not dictate the experience of your child even if you meant it for good. Parenting requires that one day, there must be a stop process. Once that process stops, there must be a discussion with the child. After the discussion, as a parent, all you can do is manage and offer advice. It was not my parent's job to make sure there was perfection in every situation. It was their job to give me the best they could each day. They did! They gave me their best and they are loved for it.

My mom and dad both have transitioned; however, laying them to rest was a moment that gave me closure that was never expected. My biggest fear of losing my dad and losing my mother is how I would react to each situation. The complexity of the relationships had changed from the time that I was a little boy to the time that now this experienced man. The man that I resented as a child had become a giant in my eyes and the woman that gave me the world had left me thinking if she liked me and that there were so many more questions that wanted to be asked and things that wanted to be said. The day my dad passed was surprising; however, the week prior, there were conversations between him and me that made it easier to bear. The last time we went to the hospital together, he told me that he was tired of coming to the hospital. Just like my dad, going to the hospital is not my favorite thing. If need be, then it would be done, but if there was a chance that we could see each other when you were released, then the one waiting on your release would be me. Dad had cancer and the radiation he did not like at all and in the conversation, there were two things that were going to happen: My dad was not going back, or my dad was going to get tired and rest. To me, there is not a chance that my dad gave up because he had to fight his whole life. This would be a fight that he felt he did not have to win, so he rested. There is something that makes me nervous when I receive a call from my sisters in the middle of the day. My brothers can call all day and there is no doubt or inkling that anything is wrong, but when my sister's number shows up, my stomach drops and I hope that they just want to talk and have no bad news. On this day, my sister called and she said the ambulance is here at the house getting ready to take your dad to the hospital. You need to come home. There was something in her voice that said she was worried. She had never been this worried when calling, but I knew that I needed to come home and for some reason, I knew that dad would not go back to the hospital. A few minutes later, she calls crying and she says that he is gone. He died in the back of the ambulance. As always, I knew it. There was a sharp pain in my chest, and it lasted for about 10 to 15 seconds. Dad was gone. The man that was now a giant in my eyes was gone. There was no feeling, there were no tears. There was a numbness that said rest, you deserve it. My dad's passing was not the hardest part for me, planning the funeral for my dad was one of the hardest things that has ever been done. In this, I learned what family thought of me, learned that no decision will be the right decision when planning a funeral, and learned that a lot of my pain came from taking care of my dad's funeral came from me wanting him to take care of me growing up. At that moment, there was a feeling of neglect, but however, I must put that to the side because, as your son, it is my responsibility to take care of you. My dad was cremated and for some of my family members, that was one of the worst things that could have happened. One of the biggest misconceptions was that the reason that he was being cremated was because I didn't want to spend the money to bury him. Besides, his son was successful, looked like he had money, and five thousand dollars would be nothing to just go to the old bank account and pull out. It was learned that just because you say you have insurance does not mean you have insurance. One of the blessings in it all was the local funeral director, who was also family or a staple in our family for years, allowed me to pay for my dad's funeral in installments; however, after a payment or two, I felt this closure need to be done and paid the complete remaining amount. When a child buries their parents, it is supposed to be expected but not expected. It has always been stated that kids bury their parents and not parents should have to bury their child. On the day of the funeral, in many of my selfish ways, I felt neglected. Neglected because, as a child, there was a feeling my dad was not there for me and now, as an adult, when the understanding of my father becomes clear and we communicated better, he was taken away. Another finish line moment that was taken away without a win. However, there has been a connection with my dad that has been with me ever since his death. The night of the day my dad was laid to rest, I began to smell cigarette smoke. My dad smoked and I did not like going over to his house because when I left the house, I would smell like smoke. On this night, the smell of my dad's house was overwhelming, so overwhelming that I asked other people did they smelled smoke and they said no. From that day until today, the smell of smoke comes and goes. The visit to the doctor, because the smoke smell has been so overwhelming, has been diagnosed as a sinus infection, imagination, and even from smoking cigars. In my heart of hearts, it's my dad letting me know that he has my back. He could not be there when I wanted him to, but he is here now. The smell still comes and goes, but now it is more of a conversation of me talking with my dad when it happens. Giants don't destroy, they build the unimaginable. Though it was not to my liking, my dad built another giant that was unimaginable. That giant is me!

Accomplishing things that are unimaginable is something that, as a generation, we do every day. Our ancestors could have never imagined some of the things we have done, seen, or accomplished. We sometimes forget that we are our ancestors' wildest dreams because of our own selfish desires and wants. For many years, I wanted to hear my mother say that she was proud of me and that I was not a disappointment to her. As an adult, I did not believe I was, but the child in me wanted to hear it because it was written, and, in my mind, it made it permanent. All of this did not matter on the last day that my mother was seen lying in her hospital bed. My mom went to the hospital and when they put her in the ambulance to take her, she gave me a hug and I said I love you. It would be the last time that I would speak to my mom, and she could speak back to me. However, on this day, I happen to go to the hospital alone. My brothers, sisters, and my aunt had been there the previous days to discuss what were the final wishes with my mother. In the room, I sat there with my mom and the sound of the machine that she was connected to, along with the contracting of her chest, was unbearable. I stayed and watched my mom, helpless and wondering all the things that had bothered me for most of my adult life. Was she proud of me? Was I a disappointment to her? Those questions would never be answered. At that moment, I stood up and hugged my mom and I apologized for not being the son that I needed to be. I told her that I was sorry if anything that was done by me disappointed her. I told her that I loved her and wished that I could have done better. If she heard me, it is not known, but I left not knowing and wishing that I could have been a better son to my mother. That night, the family was called because they were going to let my mother transition. That night, I sat home at my place and everything that was ever accomplished by me or done meant nothing. There would never be a chance to get what I needed from my mother or for her to get what she needed from me. My mom was gone and no matter what, there would be no winner.

From the cremation of my dad, his ashes have remained with me for nearly five years. It was sort of funny because knowing the question of where your dad's ashes are wanted to be asked, but no one ever did, was hilarious. Many times, I would tell him if people knew where you and I had been, they would be surprised. When mom passed, I purchased a new urn and had my dad's ashes placed in the casket with my mom. For some reason, I believe this had been discussed, whether it was jokingly with my mom or in a conversation. The family was good with it, and it was probably the easiest decision made amongst the family during my mom's funeral planning. They were back together, and there was no doubt that they loved each other, but sometimes life is better being apart. My mom was laid to rest and the song the family chose was Wind Beneath My Wings. I looked around at all the people that came to celebrate my mom and it all became clear to me who my mom was to so many folks. At that moment, memories of what my mom had done and been for so many people flashed before my eyes. This song made sense and it was the perfect song and lyrics for my mom:

It must have been cold there in my shadow.
To never have sunlight on your face
You were content to let me shine, that's your way.
You always walked a step behind

...So, I was the one with all the glory
While you were the one with all the strength
A beautiful face without a name for so long
A beautiful smile to hide the pain.

...Did you ever know that you're my hero
And everything I would like to be?
I can fly higher than an eagle.
For you are the wind beneath my wings.

...It might have appeared to go unnoticed
But I've got it all here in my heart.
I want you to know I know the truth, of course, I know
it.
I would be nothing without you.

...Did you ever know that you're my hero?
You're everything I wish I could be
I could fly higher than an eagle.
For you are the wind beneath my wings.

You will always hear me say that I am a mixture of all
my brothers' attributes. However, my character, integrity,
and empathy come from my parents. I love you, Mom &
Dad!

CJ-ism #22 - *Not until men stop seeing showing emotions as a sign of weakness will we ever be able to love our women the way they are supposed to be loved!*

Chapter 3: To the New Girl Dad

Growing up some didn't have our fathers in our lives like we wanted them to be present. Now that we have kids, we know one thing about raising kids is that everything we do for our kids is intentional. We try to make sure that they don't repeat the mistakes that we made. I know for sure that we try to make sure that they have everything that they need, in most time is everything that they want. We also know that one of the biggest things we do is try to make sure that they have the things that we didn't have growing up, whether it's physical, whether it is internal battles that we want to protect them from or whether it is the things that we learned as we grew up and didn't know we could have avoided if we had a father present. We would not have it that our children would have to learn the hard way. One difference between fatherhood is whether you have a son or a daughter. With a son, you can be direct, you can be a little rough as he gets older you can even share more of your experiences. When you have a daughter, all those rules change. The only thing you must do is (in the words of Chris Rock) keep her off the pole. It is a joke, but this has crossed every Girl's dad's mind. I'm not saying the pole is a bad thing. We just don't want it for our daughters. Seriously, when it comes to raising a daughter, the biggest thing is to protect her from you. Everything you know you got away with; you want to protect her from that. You will be the first man that she loves. You will be the first man to teach her what love looks like. Your traits and characteristics will be the foundation of her future husband. You will show her this by how you treat every woman in her life. That includes her mom that includes her aunt that includes her grandmother and even includes her friends. Your example of what she will need will all come from you. So, as a girl dad, there are three things we must be as fathers. One is that we must be accountable. Two, we must be reliable. Three, we must be consistent. These three things, I strongly believe, build trust. Trust is key to building a foundation for our kids, not that they trust everyone that they encounter, but they trust that everything we have taught them has prepared them for what they would deal with in the world. The difference between a son and a daughter is you must show boys everything because, as boys and men, we already know it all. When dealing with daughters, they are going to believe and hang on to every word that comes from their father. Whether it is their fraternal father or if it's their spiritual father. So, trusting daddy is key to being a girl dad. We must be accountable, reliable, and consistent to build that trust. Proverbs 20:7 The righteous who walks in his integrity— blessed are his children after him! In the amplified version of the bible, it states: The righteous man who walks in integrity *and* lives life in accord with his [godly] beliefs—How blessed [happy and spiritually secure] are his children after him [who have his example to follow].

Being a girl dad will by far be one of the hardest things that a man can do, but one of the biggest failures in my eyes was being a father to two amazing young men. My last relationship allowed me the privilege of being a father to my two sons. Even though, in my eyes, it was one of my biggest failures, understanding what my intent was may never be known. They will not understand the love and fear that I had for them. Stepping into fatherhood for me was exciting. There was an eagerness to form a bond and to make sure that shielding and teaching them the lessons of life was the priority. The first year in the new home, there were not really any rules set. My idea was this was a blended family and did not come in and set all the unrealistic rules when there was not really an extended knowledge of who the boys were. After the first year, from watching and learning the boys, there was a feeling that some structure was needed in the home. Being diplomatic was the first thing that came to mind. First, we, as parents, sat down and discussed what was needed. We would be a united front presenting the new rules of the home. These rules included doing schoolwork, washing dishes by 7:00 pm, waking up on Saturday morning, cleaning their upstairs bedroom and bathroom, washing their laundry, and then vacuuming the floors, preferably by 12:00 pm or 1:00 pm. After that, the day and weekend would be theirs. As a family, we sat down at the kitchen table and went over all the chores and times that they needed to be completed. The last question asked was, is there anything on this list that you do not agree with, or you would like to change? At the time, they were younger, so bedtimes for school were also included. For two years of doing this, there were no changes asked or expressed to be made.

One of the things that was not asked of the other parent was what was their idea and understanding of chores. Automatically, it was assumed that we both had the idea of chores, and this was not the case. This caused conflict in communication with the kids and with us as adults. For example, to me, the actual physical act of doing chores is useless, and the physical act of the other parent is very important. This was learned when it came time to wash dishes. Dishes were not important to me because there was a dishwasher in the house and if the act was that important, we would have used the dishwasher. There is nothing cleaner than dishes that are washed by teenagers who do not want to wash dishes. The point of washing dishes was to prioritize your time. All the times that were given were so that the kids could prioritize their day to do what they had to do so that at the proposed time, they had to be in the kitchen. One of the biggest stereotypes of black Americans is being on time. That was something that the boys would not be late in my eyes because they would know how to prioritize their time. However, on the other hand, the mother looked at the chores of dishwashing as to why they have to have a time when it is just dishes, and they can wash the dishes any time if the dishes are washed before they go to bed. Two different perspectives and, in my mind, two different opinions that were being taught. Chores and disagreements on the way the kids were raised would be an issue for the whole relationship. An issue that would lead to disrespect and the turbulence that would later take over the household.

Through all the ups and downs of trying to be a father figure there were many lessons learned. The reason that this, in my opinion, would be one of my biggest failures was because the lessons were not learned until the departure of the home was inevitable. To this day, the failure to be the true father figure that was envisioned haunts me. One of the hardest things to do is be a stepfather to children who were not biologically your kids. This is not difficult because of the kids, but it is more difficult because of the biological parent. In my heart, they were my kids—using the word stepfather makes me cringe. In the relationship it is believed that the trust needed to proper parent was not given. Not because the trust between the two of us was not there, but because there was and is a brokenness there that says the sole purpose of a mother is to protect your kids. Besides even though there was an engagement ring given, there was still not a commitment of marriage. The fear of the man leaving and damaging the kids that were or would be attached to you is still relevant and there was no reason to give total control to a man to father her children. This understanding did not come until we were separated and not in the same household. While in the house, my attitude was that it was not my job to be your friend. One of my biggest mistakes was trying to run the household like the offices—that was part of my job. Why would it not work? Leadership was me; if there was a better leader than me in my mind, we must meet one day. Structure was my purpose and if nurturing was needed, that was the mother's job. My biggest fear was that one of my sons would come home in a police car. The scenario was already played out in my mind. The police would bring them home and say that they had committed a crime in the neighborhood. They would want to take the boys or child down to the police station. It would be asked by me to the boys or child if they did what they were being accused. They would say no, and their trust would be so good with me that they would be told to go in the house, and it would be me telling the police to get the hell off my porch. Our relationship would be so well that if they came in and told me the sky was pink, there would be no reason to doubt them. That didn't happen; it went the opposite way. The communication was gone, there was no trust either way and to this day, there is a doubt that they care for me as much as the care that would have been liked for them have for me. Would they understand just what was trying to be accomplished in the world of police brutality, George Floyd, Michael Brown, Colin Kaepernick, and the movement of Black Lives Matter? My fear for their safety had caused me to create a mental prison that saw them as inmates until they received the lesson that was being taught. Trying to be the leader of the house created an outcast that was only acknowledged when something was needed or by a daughter who still saw her father as her hero regardless of what was thought by the other people living in the home. It was hard for me to win again.

In my career, my knowledge and leadership have influenced many women and men in the military and throughout the world. However, the battle in my own home was being lost. Trying to give them a father figure that they could be proud, instead, in my opinion, they received a leader of men that never communicated with children and did not understand that it was important and vital to do so. This would go on until moving out was my only option, not because of the boys but because of my health and because the respect was gone. There was no authority or structure in the house. Public enemy number one was me and living in a toxic relationship helped no one. The fear had come to the realization that a black man had joined in a relationship with a black woman, and she never really trusted him to take total control because the fear of him leaving would leave her there to pick up the pieces and heal the family again. There was no need for her to put back on her cape because she was never comfortable with taking it off. The fear of every single black mother had reared its ugly head again. This is the narrative in the black community, but the narrative of why the black man could never really be a father is rarely explored. This could not be happening; winning is what always happens in the end for me, but for some reason, this win could not be obtained. This was a lesson learned and there were many lessons from this situation.

Me: Happy Birthday, young man! Welcome to adulthood. I am proud and glad you made it to this day. I know I could be critical, strict, and even hard, but I wanted the best. I am so satisfied and know you will be a great man! I may not have done it right all the time, but a young independent man you have become. Happiest of Birthdays! You are a man now. Live your life and know if there is anything you need or need to talk about in this life journey; you can call or talk to me. One thing to remember "in life, you are not going to always get everything right; what is most important is that you made a decision, and you followed it through. The most important thing is you decide. Life is all about decisions. If it doesn't work, learn from it and keep trying, but never give up." I know it's long, but I'm proud of the man you have become and I'm no longer worried about you being ready for this world. Happy Birthday!

Child: Wow, thanks, CJ and you helped me understand things better in life and I appreciate you for that.

"I appreciate you for that" brought me to tears. Maybe they were listening; maybe it was not all in vain. The fear of this world had left and the excitement of seeing what would happen in his life had me in tears. Since moving from home, there was a realization that the common denominator in all my relationships was me. Whether it was marriage, engagement, fatherhood, or friendships, the only constant was me. So, if fixing everyone else was not an option, the only one that could be fixed was myself. Fatherhood forced me to look in the mirror, it forced me to see why statistics had included me in the number. Fatherhood made me realize that you lead at work and love at home. Leading at work creates productive individuals. Loving at home creates humans with empathy that can lead a nation to greatness. Fatherhood had forced me to therapy!

There are numerous things that were learned in therapy. However, in fatherhood it was learned that my approach to fatherhood was to give the kids everything that I missed or was not learned by me from my father. In fatherhood, it was me trying to father the little boy who was locked away in the mental prison on the way to San Antonio, Texas. The approach to fatherhood was to not be the labels that were given to me as a child and fear as a young adult. You will not be lazy, as they called me. You will not be late like every black person who believes in CP-time. You will not have a home that was not cleaned or know how to clean like mine. You will be respectful, and you will be able to look and speak to anyone while looking them in their eyes because it was fearful for me to do. You will be prepared, and no one will be able to tell you that they control what you do in your career because that is what they told me. You will be prepared for any police that approach you and you will know how to handle every situation because it was one of my biggest fears as a black man. You will know how to manage finances because no one ever taught me. Finally, you will be respectful and respected because that is what we do as black people because; for some reason, getting disrespected was ok because there was a lot of disrespect until it was learned how to be handled. This was not parenting; this was me preparing these young men to be able to handle my fears. It did not work, and it will not work. There are many things that, if time allowed, returning to correct would be a priority. Since that is impossible, there are many black men who go through the same thing, and we are quick to blame the women for making soft men and wimpy boys. Some of this may be true, but as a father who could not get it right, there are some things that were learned.

One of those things is that communication is not a one-way street. There must be two-way communication as a father. The days of do as I say and do not question what is said are gone. There must be a "Why!" Kids want to know why some things must be done. We can not take that as disrespect. We are not in a time like ours when we never question our parents. Another realization is that sometimes, no communication is the best communication for kids. Today, computers, video games, and cell phone texting dominate children's lives. They do not have time or make time to talk to their parents. However, they are listening. Sometimes, when they are not talking, it is fine because when they do ask questions, it's because they have researched or discussed it so that they can have a debate to persuade you or to tell you why it is not fair. Please put the machismo away. This generation does not classify being a man by how many sex partners one has or by how tough one may seem. Today, kids want the affection. It does not have to be physical affection, but the acknowledgement that you know what is going on and you are interested. One of the biggest mistakes that was made was not playing video games with my boys. That would have been my way of communicating with them. Playing video games is what they love to do; however, it was not my thing because the hate of losing outweighed the value of communication at the time. The opportunity was missed, and it was never recaptured. Even today, there is communication, but it is a communication of respect to you, but really, we do not know you. My first chance at fathering was finished, but it cannot be said to be a first to finish or a win.

In fatherhood, one of the hardest things that was done in my life was leaving the home and leaving my daughter behind. To me, the relationship was toxic; there would be days and sometimes months with no real conversation from anyone but my five-year-old daughter. Many times, the thought of just riding the relationship out was my plan. Not until after the repeated trips to the emergency room with heart problems and palpitations did a doctor make it plain to me. She said, "Your heart is strong and there is no problem with your heart; however if you do not remove the stress in your life, it will become a problem!" At that point, it was known that a decision had to be made. Once employment was found, the decision was made to move to Raleigh. The hard part was knowing that my daughter would not be going with me. In my mind, she was in the best place at the time and that was with her mother. She has a great mother, and her mother would be the most impressionable of her at this time. There was no idea as to how much this would affect my daughter. My daughter is shy and quiet, like the little boy who was put away on the way to basic training. Yet, her voice is very loud when she speaks. God has given me another opportunity to get it right and the thought of leaving makes me doubt if the path that was chosen was the right path. Having a daughter puts life in perspective for a man. You automatically become the protector. The only thing that you know to protect her from is you. Your experiences, your wrongs, and your relationships have given you all the tools to protect her from you. It puts into perspective how good of a person you were in relationships.

There is not a more difficult feeling than your daughter telling you that she is mad at you because you left however, she is too young to understand why. That is a feeling that you will have to carry until you are able to explain. Once you can explain, you have to hope and pray that she believes it because you are the last to give an explanation. There was a time when it was said by me that there was no way that leaving my child would be an option. This is a prime example of having your ego judge people without knowing all the facts and being ready to point the finger. Even though most of the separation with my daughter has been amicable with her mother, there are times that it is understood why some men leave. It has nothing to do with the child however, it can be that the other parent had made it more difficult to be around the environment. There is and has always been a problem with conflict resolution when it comes to black men in relationships. Often, we are given the moniker of deadbeat, cheater, or lazy because of some of our actions. In very few instances, some have asked the fathers why they are not there. If you were to go down your social media feeds, there would be so many posts of father bashing and how the man is no good and not present in the child's life. It is rare that you will see men speak badly about the mother of their child if they are a good or bad mother. Why is that? In my opinion, most men understand that what is said about their kids' mothers will be repeated and it will be used as a weapon in some form or another. The truth of the matter is that most men leave because they do not want to be with the mother and it's hard for the mother to understand, so she makes it hard for the father to parent. Sometimes, the moniker of a strong black woman is a threat to having a strong black family, which makes it hard to have a strong black father, whether he is in or out of the house.

The daughter and father relationship suffers because of this, and it is up to the fathers to be strong enough to stand in the fire so that the relationship does not suffer and patterns are not repeated. It is important so that you can protect your daughter from the experiences and mistakes that you made as a man. There were a few reasons as to why leaving my daughter was necessary. There are also reasons that were caused by me and there are reasons where being selfish and not knowing how to communicate and problem-solve correctly made it difficult for both parents to live. My goal as a girl dad is to make sure that my daughter can recognize love in all forms. My goal is to make sure my daughter knows that her validation does not come from a man. My goal is to make sure that my daughter knows that her voice should never be silenced and that when she speaks it does not come from hate or any other selfish places. My goal for my daughter is to love God first. Finally, my goal as a father to my daughter is to have her Win! To Win, and not let society determine what is a win, but her convictions, hard work, goals, and determination dictate her success. As parents, it is our job to make sure the little young girl gets the chance to grow into a woman without having to suppress any part of whom she is to become.

CJ-ism #25 - *Sometimes, we don't realize that the shoes we wear are much bigger than what the size says!*

DETERMINATION

CJ-ism #3 - *When you think what you do isn't enough, stop worrying about what other people think!*

Chapter 4: You Were Not Put Here to Fail

Let me reintroduce myself, my name is Clarence Jones, a black man raised in Franklinton, NC and I was not put here to fail. My number one job is being a father. I served 20 years in the greatest Air Force in the world, The United States Air Force. Pursuing my education has allowed me to achieve three degrees. The only difference between us, is stepping out of the box! Stepping outside of the box is not anything new. There are many that step outside the box. However, for everyone who steps outside the box, there are probably ten who are afraid to step out or are comfortable inside the box. Regardless of what your box may be, eventually, we all will have to step outside the box. What is the box? This box is a representation or symbol of the state you are in now or something that you may be scared to achieve or try to achieve. Many people get in the box by being born in the box, experiencing failure, being comfortable, or not seeing anything in life outside the box.

Five components that allow you to be successful outside the box or your comfort zone are education, dress, being courteous, confidence, and vision. We must educate ourselves. Many times, when we say education, many people think of going to a four-year institution for a degree. The simple fact is we should be receiving some type of education every day. This can occur through reading, having conversations with other people and listening. Anything we do to better ourselves can be considered education. Our dress is also important. Dress for the job you want or the event that you are attending. How you dress says a lot about how you adapt to certain situations. This determines, in some cases, if anyone is going to take you seriously. There was a battle rapper that was excellent, in my opinion. He won a battle rap, and everyone was speaking about him. He would wear a suit and tie to every battle rap. However, after that initial battle rap, other rappers slaughtered him. It wasn't because he could not rap. They used the way he dressed to drop bars upon bars against him. Nothing he said held much weight because all the attention had been used and placed on the way he dressed. In my opinion, this was a prime example of dressing the part. Regardless of which type of room you are a part. If you do not dress the part, many people will not take you seriously. Confidence! What is confidence? In life, there are a lot of people that have confidence. Often, they do not have self-confidence. What is the difference? Confidence is supported by experience and external evidence. Self-confidence is about the belief and trust you have in yourself. We have the tendency to learn and be experts at our jobs to the point that we become prisoners of our jobs. We get so comfortable that we create boxes even in our success. Because we are comfortable, we start to believe that we cannot do any other job better than we can do the job we have been doing for so many years. In 2012, I retired from the military. In the Air Force, before retiring, most people attend a class called TAP, which stands for Transition Assistance Program. In this class, it prepares you for transitioning from the military to the civilian sector. While attending this class there was an experience with another military member. He sat beside me and was in a panic about what was his next career. He had met his high-year tenure, but he had no clue as to what he wanted to do at the end of his career. He asked, "Why are you not nervous about getting out of the military?"

I told him, "I always knew that twenty years would be enough for me. My problem was not knowing what to do after twenty years. My problem was trying to get to twenty years with the current fitness standards."

He then looked and said, "You must already have a job."

"No," I exclaimed. "It is just that I knew this day would come and there would be no issue in finding a job." He still just sat there and looked because he had no idea where he was going to go and fuel airplanes. He had lost confidence in his skills, and he had lost confidence that he had done the work to do another job. This sergeant was defeated before he even left the military. There was no doubt in my mind that his lack of confidence would turn into desperation once the final day came of his military career. There was no vision. We all must have a vision. The vision to see ourselves doing better. Along with that vision comes the ability to speak it into existence. One of the most harmful parts of our bodies is our tongue. Many people do not understand how much we manifest by speaking negative thoughts in our minds into existence. With your vision, speak life into yourself and your situations. What you put into your mind and what you speak through your mouth is what you get out of life. You deserve everything that you can imagine and work for in your mind and through preparation. Just because you cannot see it in the natural with your eyes does not mean you cannot see it at all. What you envision, you can achieve.

After being familiar with these five components you must take advantage of opportunities. One of my biggest flaws is that networking is not something that interested me and not something that was high on my radar. There has always been a mentality that doing it alone is possible. It's not. No one achieves success alone. You can be successful, but everyone needs someone to be successful. Taking advantage of opportunities builds your foundation. The number of opportunities you take advantage of determines how strong your foundation will be in life, career, and self-perseverance. The biggest stigmas that cause me and many like me not to take advantage of opportunities are pride, selfishness, and the fear that someone is going to be able to say that they helped you or are the reason that you succeeded. We want to be responsible for our own success. We are responsible; however, we are responsible for our failures. Most times, we fail by ourselves. There has never been anyone bragging about helping you fail. Most may tell how they helped you succeed. The main goal is that we succeeded, however we focus on the chatter of someone taking credit. We need to realize we succeeded or are succeeding and if that means you get a piece of the credit, then so be it. We have accomplished our goal of succeeding. Stepping outside of your box allows you access to many things, such as; opportunities, jobs, education, the arts, and notoriety. Any time you can better who you are as a person, you should step outside the box. Stepping outside the box in any situation allows you to do three things continuously. It allows you to keep thinking, believing, and dreaming.

I AM A DREAMER

MY DREAMS ARE REAL

THE ONLY THING STOPPING MY DREAMS

IS FEAR

AND FEAR IS

MY DOUBTS TELLING MY DREAMS

I CANNOT DO IT.

BUT I WILL STEP OUTSIDE OF THE BOX

BECAUSE MY FOUNDATION IS STRONG

AND MY FOUNDATION WILL SOON BE THE
NORM. SO TODAY

I AM PREPARING

TO TAKE MY FIRST STEP

OUTSIDE THE BOX!

This poem was written while sitting at my sister's house shortly after retiring from the military. Fresh off a divorce and not knowing where my next place of living would be was one of the most uncomfortable positions that was ever experienced in my life at this time. I spent twenty years in the military to end back up in Franklinton, NC, at my sister's house with no direction. Life could not be this cruel. So, one day before doing my daily resume submission and heading to the golf course for my daily whipping, by three older gentlemen, those words were written.

Failure is determined by the individual. No one can tell you what failure is to you. We have this notion that if it's not first place, it is failure. The experience means nothing, the lessons learned mean nothing, or the individuals you impacted mean nothing. Oftentimes, failure is given to us by what society thinks is failure. What has been learned in my failures can look like success to many people. As well as, my successes can look like failures to many people. While in the military, my goal was to retire at twenty years with the rank of Master Sergeant or above. Not once did my goal in the military was to be a great leader. In my mind, achieving the rank of Master Sergeant automatically established that you are a great leader. This could not be further from the truth; however, it is still to this day the standard of what a great leader is in the military in some cases. If the comparison of military careers with the group of friends that the journey began and ended with was compared to my career was based on rank. There is no doubt that it would be a failure. Everyone that did 20 years or more in the military that was part of my first base had achieved no less than the rank of Master Sergeant. There were a few more than three that had achieved the rank of Chief Master Sergeant. It was a few friends who treated me differently because the rank of

Master Sergeant was not achieved, but nonetheless, they were great friends. The ironic part about this is if we took the same group of people and said how many people did you influence and continue to influence today, there is no doubt in my mind that there are not more than three that have had more influence than me. This is not a comparison of anyone's skills, but it is to show that how we determine success can be detrimental to all that we accomplish. It shows that if we continue to determine failure and success by what people see on the outside, such as rank, titles, or office size, then we will continue to miss out on what success really means. All these things are great to have and great to achieve, but they do not determine if you are successful or not if that is not your goal.

As a young child outside hitting rocks with a stick as if it were a baseball bat, there was a voice, to me, it was the voice of God that said, "You were not put here to fail." It was clear, it was loud in my head, and it was present. This one sentence, you were not put here to fail, has sustained me all my life. This was a promise made to me and regardless of what happens, it is known by me that I was not put here to fail. There were times when the conclusion was that it was a failure. This sentence was questioned. Not making rank in the military, it was questioned. Divorce, it was questioned. Promotions on the job it was questioned. Turned down from jobs, it was questioned.

The questioning of you were not put here to fail was so rampant that it made me analyze what is the definition of failure. Robert Greene, in the book Mastery, describes two kinds of failure.

He states: There are two kinds of failure. The first comes from never trying out your ideas because you are afraid or because you are waiting for the perfect time. This kind of failure you can never learn from, and such timidity will destroy you. The second kind comes from a bold and venturesome spirit. If you fail in this way, the hit that you take to your reputation is greatly outweighed by what you learn. Repeated failure will toughen your spirit and show you with absolute clarity how things must be done. In fact, it is a curse to have everything go right on your first attempt. You will fail to question the element of luck, making you think that you have the golden touch. When you do inevitably fail, it will confuse and demoralize you past the point of learning. In any case, to apprentice as an entrepreneur, you must act on your ideas as early as possible, exposing them to the public, a part of you even hoping that you'll fail. You have everything to gain.

He also states: What scares me more than failure is not trying. I can live with failure. I can't live with not trying. The former allows me to sleep; the latter keeps me awake.

There is nothing more dangerous than a man who has healed himself!

Unknown

Chapter 5: Just To Be Loved

Today, I looked at a picture of my ex-wife. Why? Thank you for asking. I cannot give you an answer. Since my divorce, there has always been this want for a conversation. Not that it is for closure. That is something that was received years ago. My reason was and is because, in the last months of my marriage, it did not seem as if the talks, arguments, actions, or lies were something that was ever imagined by the lady that I fell deeply in love with on that special wedding day. Was it post-traumatic stress syndrome, was it that she lost confidence in me as a husband, did she really think there was jealousy for her career, or was there really someone else? I look for answers because that is something that was never received. Did there have to be an answer for closure? Closure is something that was received a long time ago. Deep down inside, I feel that as her husband, as her ex-husband, that is something that was deserved.

For some reason every woman that I truly loved, there was always an obstacle or event that was left unanswered. Not until my last relationship did a conversation have to be had with myself. From that conversation, there were a few things that were realized about me. One is that I have a pride and stubbornness that needed to be checked and who better to check it besides me? Two, that trust was a big issue. In my reflection or self-evaluation, it was realized that trusting was an issue for me because, deep down there was a feeling that I was not good enough. Even though there was not much to offer in my eyes, there was always a thought that there was an ulterior motive as to why the person who was with me loved me. Most of the time, the relationships were doomed from the start because of my thinking. Another thing that was realized is my self-esteem was fake. It was a shadow confidence and the little boy that left years ago was still in there yearning for acceptance. However, as the grown man, there was acceptance. More than I could ever want, but it was manufactured, and the persona was about to have a real conversation with the little boy. Finally, there was the realization that I had died for everyone except myself. Forgiveness for me was never hard, forgetting was the hardest part. However, when it came to me, there was no forgiveness for the bad checks that were written, there was no forgiveness for the women's hearts that were broken, there was no forgiveness for lies that were told to put on a façade of who Clarence really was in life, there was no forgiveness for not being a model son. Literally, I had not died to myself to live the actual life that was being lived. On the outside, my life was one to be proud of, but inside, there were battles that were going on that could only be solved by me in my mind. Without the skills to harness these battles, the only thing that harnessed these battles was women, sex, and love. If I was loved, I was fine; however, by loving me, there was the possibility that all the women that were encountered through sex and love, I was destroying.

"There is nothing more dangerous than a man who has claimed to heal himself." This is a quote from an unknown person. When it was read or seen, instantly, the label of dangerous came to my mind. That was me dangerous. Today, a lot of men do not know how dangerous we are when it comes to marriage, fatherhood, or self-evaluation. Speaking with friends and some of the young men who call for advice and mentorship, it was realized that we have no idea who we are in certain situations. Overall, we know who we are as people, but when it comes down to individual relationships, in some areas, we are clueless. This stems, in my opinion, from the false narrative that if you have the basics down, car, house, and partner, you have succeeded. What we do not realize is the little boy or young man who was hurt or even destroyed in some situations is still yearning to be loved. Many times, in these relationships, we leave not because we do not want to stay, we leave because we do not know how to fix or communicate with the person in the relationship, how to love ME! We do not know how to love ourselves and that makes it hard to communicate it, so we leave because the war inside does not allow us the peace we need to receive love or even give love. At the end of the day, all we ever want is to be loved, we just do not know how to communicate it.

After my self-evaluation, part of my process was the 5-why method. Why was I asked these hard questions to myself that even made me stop at times and say this is bullshit and call someone else to come over and give me the love that I thought I needed. Sexual relationships were something that had never been a problem for me when I realized that the women really liked this persona. When it came to pride and stubbornness, it is something that was received honestly. All my uncles were proud men. There was a confidence and slight arrogance to them all. This not only came from my dad's side of the family, but it also was prevalent on my mother's side of the family. So, for many years, if confidence was not had, however, you did not know it. My pride would not let you see it. It was the beginning of internal battles with pride that was so powerful that, as a young kid, I was willing to go hungry instead of risking my pride. One day, while home with my mom, constantly there were complaints about being hungry from me. Many times, my mom told me to call my dad because she did not have any money. Still, the complaining did not stop. Looking back at it today, I have never even been close to hunger, but in my mind, I was two stomach growls from buzzards flying over my head. Finally, my mom said, "I do not have any money, but look in my pocketbook and get the book of food stamps and go to Piggly Wiggly and get some hotdogs." Immediately, my pride kicked in. There was no way you would be sending me to a store with food stamps and risk some of my friends from school seeing me at the counter with food stamps. That will not happen. I refused to go. The look of disbelief that was seen on my mom's face I can still see today. However, then, to me, the look was boy take these stamps. Now I see it as a how dare you refuse to go the store with food stamps after I work daily to feed you and you have the audacity to say no to going to a store with food stamps. You can eat the food that I purchase with food stamps, but instead of being seen, you will go hungry because of food stamps. That day, she realized how prideful her son was, and she never gave me any reason to think that food stamps were too good for me or my family. Her face said it all, but at that time, my pride did not care. The pride and stubbornness would travel with me throughout my younger and adult years. It would manifest itself through arguments in relationships. If I was right, there was no way one could tell me that I was wrong. If there was a belief that embodied what was believed, then there was no way that the belief could be changed. This was dangerous because it caused me to believe that success could be achieved alone. The pride and stubbornness made me believe that no help or advice was needed from anyone to be successful. After a self-evaluation, it was realized that one could achieve success in many instances. However, one will never be successful doing it alone. In the end, it was detrimental to my military career and to my marriage.

In my marriage, one of my biggest regrets is that we did not fight hard enough for our marriage to survive. Many thoughts of did we both want it or if we were on a seesaw each day where one person wanted it more than the other. My pride caused me not to accept the olive branch when it was given. At the end of my marriage, there was a lot of disdain for my ex. One day, there was a call and at the end of the call was a storage company. The guy from the storage company said, "Is this Clarence Jones? We have some items in storage for you and if you do not come and get these items by Friday at four o'clock pm, then you will forfeit these items and they will be discarded. "Flabbergasted, I exclaimed," What do you mean my items will be thrown in the trash and why do you have my items? It is Wednesday morning and I work the third shift and you expect me to make it to DC by Friday and pick up items? How am I supposed to do that?" He said, "That is not my problem. Your ex-wife said that you would come get them and we need them out by Friday. You will need a small U-Haul truck to get the items." He gave me his name and his number and told me to call when details were available for pickup. Immediately the call was made to my ex with no answer. There would be no answer until Friday when my items were retrieved. After coordinating with my job to get time off from work and zero luck in finding a U-Haul in Washington, DC, on the weekend with one day's notice, the drive to DC was being made without knowing what was going to happen. After arriving at the storage place, the storage guy seemed very disgusted and rude to me. We went to retrieve all the items that would fit into my SUV and then it was time to go inside to sign. As we both were adding signatures, it was noticed that he was covering up an address. Curious, so I asked, "Why are you covering up the address?"

He stated, "Your ex-wife stated that she has a restraining order against you and that you could not come to her place."

"What?" I said, looking surprised. "The address is…," I said. "You do not have to hide it; we haven't spoken in months. She told you that so that you would bring these items back. There is not restraining order, why would there be? Is this why you are acting so rude?" I asked.

"Yes," he said. "We are doing you a favor."

"No, you did her a favor. She lied to you," I spoke. After signing the papers, he apologized and said that he was wrong for doing that without knowing both sides or just believing her side.

Driving down the road, it was a blur on both sides. A restraining order, why would she say this? As I drove, I called still with no answer. The message that was left said, "A restraining order, you told the people that you had a restraining order on me? It's enough that we are divorcing, you are trying to damage my character. This is a new low, and I am speechless. A restraining order! Wow!" It was probably one of the hardest days of my life, on the interstate, I pulled over and cried. It hurt that much because not knowing who this person was, in my heart, there was still a belief that it was not the person that I married. After getting myself together, there was a call made to a friend who had counseled us as a couple in the past. She could tell that there was something wrong and she asked what was wrong. I explained everything about the storage and the supposed restraining order. She asked me if I was sure that they said a restraining order because that seemed crazy. Yes, I am sure I said I have the paper in my hand, and it says hold for restraining order. She said to throw it out the window. Do not let that energy get to you and she immediately started to pray for us both. At this point afterward, there was peace, but I knew that it would be hard to trust or put belief in anyone as I had put into this lady. A few minutes later, my ex called and acted like everything was fine. In a calm voice, I asked why you told the storage people that you had a restraining order against me. She said she did not say that and for some reason, it did not matter. I knew that she was lying. Regardless of what we go through, there will be nothing that I would do to try to destroy you or your character and you told them there was a restraining order. You could have told me so that there could have been arrangements for me to pick up all my items. Instead, you told them there was a restraining order and I had two days to get off work and find a way to get my items. You also kept the Thomas Blackshear pieces and you know we both have certain items. I am so disappointed, but it's okay. She still said that she did not say that, but I didn't believe it and she hung up. This was one of the points that made me forever regret being a good man to anyone.

There is something to be said about a man who has been betrayed. Even though there are women who are betrayed by men daily, when it comes to a man being betrayed, it hurts his soul. Emotional pain for a man is by far the worst kind of pain a man can feel. It is even worse when it comes from someone he loves. Especially if the someone he loves is a significant other, it destroys him. When we are destroyed emotionally, the road to recovery may take years. Finding someone of the opposite you can trust is the most satisfying trait that a man can have in a partner. It is not the sex, looks, or money that one possesses but trust. If a man trusts a woman, he can be vulnerable, he can be weak, he can be strong and he can be himself around the woman with whom he is spending time. This, by far, is the most fulfilling thing in a relationship for a man, in my opinion. The battles that we have as men require trust that allows us to empty our emotions to our spouse and then return to the world outside our homes and be productive. The allowing of a man to be able to pour out his emotions also allows him to provide comfort and attention to the woman to receive and protect the woman when she is vulnerable and just wants to be held. Most times, the battles we face, we war with them daily and when we cannot come home and release the battles we face in a good environment, it does not allow us to refill with the nurturing that women provide. As a man, we do not have time to add more of what you are giving because we are full. We are an emotional time bomb with a fuse that we try to put out and not explode at home. This is a place of rest, but most of the time, it becomes a battlefield of two people who love fighting each other because neither has room to be poured into at the end of the day.

On March 16, 1992, there was a decision made in my life that would change my life forever. This decision was made on my way to San Antonio, Texas while taking my first-ever plane ride to becoming a man in the United States Air Force. The decision that was made over thirty thousand feet in the air was that today, Clarence Jones would not be who he was but there would be a young man that was confident, not afraid of anything, and a person that had all things together. This is the beginning of a persona that could not die, it was the beginning of putting the little shy, black kid in the background. It was the beginning of CJ. One can say there was a shyness that was had if you were not known by me growing up. The little quiet one until you were known, then slowly, the shell would be removed. Around my friends from home, I was considered the smart one, sometimes funny, and the one who was the voice of reasoning in most cases. Many times, there would be nights that repeatedly I would write my name in cursive as if it were the signature of an autograph. Even today, there are times that I catch myself writing my name in cursive to practice for the time that fame would approach me. On this night, all my cares, shyness, and insecurities would be left behind. This is the night that the little boy who lived inside was put in a room and not allowed to come out unless he was alone with himself.

Women were never an issue for me for two reasons—one was because, growing up, there were no women or girls interested in me during school or college. Secondly, because in the 90s, dark-skinned brothers were such a commodity that with a little bit of looks, style, and personality, someone would give you a chance. Wesley Snipes was my modern-day hero. Even though it seems as if colorism is what my self-esteem was based on, it could not be further from the truth. The truth is that not too many women were checking for dark-skinned brothers in the 80s and the beginning of the 90s. This is something that was used to my advantage and if you knew me, then it was known that every bit of the advantage was used. This manufactured self-esteem and newfound attractiveness made me feel untouchable to an extent. There were nightly and weekly escapades that would be too unreal to be true. However, with each conquer of women there was an emptiness. Never were their relationships, only sex and the opportunity to see you again. Past insecurities did not allow me to make relationships a priority. If it was a priority, the women that there truly were feelings either used my kindness as a weakness or told me that it was only a friend-with-benefits situation. In all the fun, there was one woman who there were truly feelings. This woman, we never had sex. We would go out to dinner and watch what we called chick flicks at her home. At this time, there was no transportation for me, but she would pick me up and bring me home, only to find out when she returned me home or after leaving from driving a friend's car and later purchasing my own, she would have a man over that she was sleeping with during the time that I left. In my mind, we were getting to know each other, and the popular guy had calmed down and was not sleeping with anyone. Not until it was found out that she had gotten married did it become a realization to me that I was not the one. This would not only happen once with this person, but the Mr. Get Who He Wants had the same thing happen twice with the same lady. That is how much I cared for this woman. Neither time was there a phone call to say, "Hey CJ, I am getting married. This was found out through a mutual friend, who had no idea that the relationship we had going on was more serious than either of us had led to believe. At the end of the day, it was hidden because it was only a relationship that was being had alone. This devastated me and it only increased the number of women that was being intimate with me and most of all, it put all the pain that was in that moment and placed it in the hands of that little boy who was put in the closet, only coming out when it was just him dealing with himself. Relationships would be ruled out from this point on until marriage became a possibility. For nine years, there were many women who were misled. There were many women who thought he was such a gentleman, and there were many women who thought that one day we would be together. However, in the back of my mind, there would never be a woman who would take me to the point of disappointment or hurt again. This caused me to miss out on some great women that was marriage material. One woman was a younger woman, with beautiful dark skin and I know she cared for me more than I cared for myself. We would see each other nearly every day, and, in my mind, there was an unsettling feeling that bothered me because all that was known to me was that one day, she would be hurt or disappointed by me. We still talked and messed around and enjoying her company was always a pleasure, but we never made it official. There would be times that the infamous "Black Ice" would perform his strip show for her to the group 112 song. Truly, I enjoyed her but trying not to hurt someone when you are hurting only cause you to destroy the person emotionally. They never know what to think and they constantly wait for you to decide. One day, my way out happened. Orders were received for me to return to Pusan, Korea. This would be my second tour to South Korea, and this would be my way out of being in a relationship but not being with her. My plan was to go to South Korea and then date from Korea. This was a way that the relationship would not end, but at the same time, being in Korea would not stop me from being the me that was created by me. We sat down one night, and we discussed what we would do. At the time, I asked her if she would wait for me to come back from Korea and without hesitation, she said yes. Everything that was wanted by me, but at that moment the little boy grabbed at my consciousness. In my mind, there was a battle that said she is younger than you, you would allow her to wait for you and you know even when you return, the possibility of you all being together will be slim to none. How could you hurt someone this vulnerable and need to experience life on her own terms? Instantly, I told her that I did not want her to wait. She did not want to hear it and cried, but in my heart of hearts, it was the right thing to do. My decision made her mad and even to this day, we joke about it, but there is no doubt that she cared for me enough to wait. There is no telling what we could have been, but we remain great friends and we joke that her son will marry my daughter one day and the irony will be on us.

Hurt people, hurt people. The day that I decided not to be who I was was the day that was decided that every woman that was encountered would be hurt by me. What was realized is that most men who have women hand over fist are men who have a little boy inside who is hurting and is afraid of being healed. How do you heal a little boy in a grown man's body is the question. Everyone's answer is different; however, healing the little boy within required me to die to myself. There was a sermon that was heard by me a time ago and in the sermon, the preacher said that one had to die daily to live forever. Dying meant asking forgiveness of your sins, doing a daily self-evaluation of your daily activities and doing anything that was not of

God. You needed to repent and die in your flesh daily. For many years, while lying in bed at night, my prayer would be to forgive me for my sins and forgive me if, during the day, there was someone who was hurt, insulted, or misunderstood me. This became the norm until it was realized that all the forgiveness in the world could be asked, but inside of me, there was a little boy who was hidden from the world and not once was forgiveness asked for locking him within. This little boy never died, nor did this little boy have the opportunity to heal. This little boy was alive and, at this point, still felt all the hurt and pain, plus the added pain he had added to himself as a grown man. This little boy was the reason that being loved would be impossible. He was the reason that when things were not right, he went back to the closet. He was the reason that communication was an issue because being able to express himself was never an option. He was the reason that he could not trust because he was never allowed to trust himself in any situation. The little boy was the reason that love was so distant because he didn't receive self-love and hid the emotion by loving woman after woman, leaving a path of destruction. Finally, the grown man realized that love would not be viable until he died for the little boy and forgave himself for locking himself into the closet. It would not happen until he forgave himself for adding all the hurt he received and placing more and more on him to carry. Forgiving the little boy inside of us

120

requires us to die to the grown man's flesh and heal the hurt that we have placed on the little boy in the closet. Forgiveness is powerful; however, it is liberating when you can forgive yourself. Through my journey of forgiving myself, it is hard to believe that anyone could have loved me. There wasn't the ability in me that would allow me to love. Searching for love to fulfill me when the place that love would reside was already filled by a little boy who experienced a large amount of hurt. After many years of hurting, being hurt, and hurting people, there comes a time when love must prevail. Loving yourself is only second to loving God and once you learn how to love yourself, you can truly love the person you are with or the person that will soon be the Ying to your yang.

Until you have walked in my shoes

You can never ever sing my blues.

Oh, never sang my blues.

And until you have felt the pain of a broken man

You can never start to understand why I think this way.

Why I am starting to lose my faith.

Have a little mercy!

Show a little mercy!

Give a little mercy!

Just a little mercy!

Until we make a change

Everything that's wrong remains the same.

Lord knows, remain the same.

And until, until love has it way.

Then and only then there will be better days

There will be better days.

Have a little mercy!

Show a little mercy!

Give a little mercy!

Just a little mercy!

Mercy by Anthony Hamilton

After you have traveled the road of love and hit every dead end there was during the travel, traveling the road again is highly unlikely. It makes you question ever falling or being in love again. It makes you revisit the question of "What is love?" This is probably one of the few questions that is subjective and can be right even when it is wrong. There have been times that love for me was a beauty, there have been times when love for me was sex, there were times when love for me was family and there have been times that love for me was for acceptance. In all these instances, my loving each of these traits or actions was right. No one can tell you what love is to you. At the same time, your love could be totally wrong to the next person. Loving someone requires mercy. It is a necessity for love to survive. We are all broken vessels pieced back together with the glue of life lessons. We do not know each other's story and we do not know how much it has taken to rebuild the vessel you have chosen. Some of us are fragile, some are forged by fire. Regardless of how we were put back together, we all require special handling. Do you want to be handled? If you do, are there special instructions and do you know how to communicate those instructions? If you do not want to be handled, where do you reside to sit alone by yourself in a safe space from ever being broken again? How safe is the space in which you reside? Is there a fear or a need for you to be held again?

Just to be loved is what everyone wants, but how you want to be loved and communicate that becomes the problem. Can you be a protector, can you be a provider, can you be a friend? Will you allow someone to protect, provide, or be a friend to you? One of the things that was realized was that, in most cases, my relationship characteristics as a man were that of a traditionalist. The man is the head of the house. He provides, he is the leader, and he protects his home. Everything that enters the home comes in through the head, whether it is physical or spiritual. As a man, you are to protect your home spiritually and physically. Many times today, this is seen as a bad thing about being a traditionalist. Traditionalism does not always mean the woman being submissive, the man paying all the bills, or the woman cooking all the time. It means that there are roles and that each one has a role, and each role must be respected by the other person. If your spouse is good with finances, why not let her or him handle the finances? If your husband enjoys cooking, why not let him take over some of the cooking duties? It's about compromise and realizing each other strengths to make the union work. How do we get there? Is it too late?

As a husband, a fiancé' or a boyfriend, there is a feeling that loving hard in all these situations has really caused me to rethink if relationships are something that will be in my future. In all the situations, the need to win and the need to have the perfect wife and kids has caused me to rethink the need to love because all the wins ended in hurt. The urge just to be loved is never dying and being loved is vital for any human to survive. One must be loved—traveling the road again in this search for love; the fragility remains; however, it does not discourage. The thirst for companionship urges on, but not just anyone can quench the thirst. Many times, the need to be touched still shows strong, but it does not leave emptiness.

CJ-ism # 44 – *Never Compromise Who You Are for What You Do!*

CJ-ism # 37 - *Your journey is your story; you can change it to your liking. So, if you are in a situation change the story.*

Chapter 6: Being A Black Man in America

L.A.U.G.H. Listen, ask, understand, guide, and hug. In the toughest part of my life, this is what I had to do to maintain my mental health. So many times, as a black man in America, we forget to L.A.U.G.H. We are taught, we teach, and we learn to make our situations work. In 2012, I retired from the United States Air Force. The ironic part about my life and retiring from the military was that February 7, 2012, was my last day in the US Air Force. On February 7, 2005, I married the love of my life, and finally, on February 7, 2012, my divorce was final to the love of my life. The common thing on each of those February 7 was that it was a day of crying and a day of emotional instability. Growing up there was never this moment where I thought that life would be easy for me scenario. There was always this feeling that you would succeed, but for you to succeed, you will go through a storm to get there. You may be small in stature at the time, but what you are going through will build your muscle. This muscle was not the physical muscle but the mental muscle. As a black man, there are many days that giving up was a viable option. Giving up was not an option because of inadequateness. Giving up was an option because, mentally, the strain of proving yourself every day took a toll on who you were as a man. There are three areas has been the hardest mentally for me. Those areas that affected my mental health the most are relationships, fatherhood, and career.

For me, marriage was one of the highlights of my life. Relationships have always been by far the best situations for me to be in as a man. Marriage for seven years and cohabitating for four years was an experience in some days is missed and some days, the thanks for not being there is a blessing. When discussing relationships with friends, males and females, there are many reasons why each other thinks that relationships do not work. However, for the men, most of the reasons remain consistent. There are three things that are non-negotiable for me in my life at this age. Those three things are respect, peace, and intimacy, not particularly in that order, but in that order. When we briefly look at the three, we even see them different when it comes to men and women.

As stated before, part of my life, I was married for seven years. In my marriage, my wife gave me the respect that I felt I needed. How this played out in her mind could have been totally different, but when it came to respect, it was always there until the end of the marriage. In the marriage, the man of the house was me. If there was a final decision that needed to be made, I made it. If there was something that I did not feel that she needed to do, she did not do it. If there was a situation that I felt that we needed to accomplish before some other tasks were started, we did it. Do not get me wrong, we both made decisions and most of the decisions were hers, but there were some decisions that I felt strongly about and did not feel a compromise needed to be met. The decision was on my shoulders. There were never any questions and there was never any "I told you so!" There was never a question of what place I held in the tier of marriage, regardless of status, income, emotions, surrounding, or environment. This made it easy to be a husband. This made it easy to love my wife. The respect she showed made loving unconditionally easy because, at the end of the day, respect says to a man, I have your back, even when you are not my favorite person. It even says from a man's point of view, because I know you respect me, if you are not in a place of loving me or liking me at the time, I am going to do all that I have to do to make sure I keep you in a place to love me because I *NEED* you to respect me. In my opinion, respect is a need of every man, especially of every black man. If there were ingredients in the male ego, those ingredients would be respect, peace, intimacy, and confidence. The male ego is shattered because one or more of these ingredients are missing. Respect in a relationship also works totally differently if it is not received in a relationship. Without respect in a relationship, you are fertilizing a breeding ground for resentment, infidelity, turmoil, and stress in the relationship. In most of the jobs that I have worked, there has been the respect of most of my employees, peers, and some white men. Still nothing can be more disheartening than to work all day and to come home and to not have the respect that you deserve or feel you deserve as a man in your own home. Whether it is deserved or not, the key is to feel the respect you deserve as a man in your own home. The last couple of years that was lived with my ex-fiancé', I resented coming home. It wasn't because we did not have a nice home. It wasn't because there was no love in the home at the time. It wasn't because it was not a comfortable place to be physically. The reason was because of all the things that had gone on throughout the day. As the car turned into the neighborhood, the closer to my home I drove, it seemed the more and more every bit of power and authority that was had as a man was leaving my body. This was not a power of control; this was a power of what you long to be as a man. As a man, there is this dream of being a provider and when you come home, this is your castle. There is a level of respect that is given that is not asked for because it is unspoken that you are husband, you are dad, you are king of your castle. For me, that was taken away, so when the arrival for me pulled into the driveway, there was a level of anxiety and stress that resulted in hospital visits and chest pains. This was not because of anyone else's fault but because of the lack of preparation for being a man and not being able to communicate your feelings.

Growing up, money has never been a motivator for my success. However everything that has been loved by me has been destroyed by money directly or indirectly. If there was a way to survive in this world without the need for money, in the front of the line would be me.

The goal in America is to have the house, the car, the wife, the children, and the white picket fence. In the America that I live it is attainable, but never something that was wanted. When I retired from the military, there were nearly twenty-eight countries that were visited by me. Of those twenty-eight countries, there were only three of those countries that were visited, and the feeling of being less of a man was felt. Those three countries were Greece, Spain, and the United States of America. Let's talk about the good US of A. There is a love-hate relationship that many of us have with America. By far, it is one of the best countries in the world. However, it is by far one of the worst countries that I have ever experienced.

The first country that was ever visited by me was South Korea. It was February of 1996 and I arrived in Seoul, South Korea. There was not an inkling of a clue as to where my next stop would be or how I would get to my next stop. There was one thing prevalent and that was the people were nice and were intrigued by me. Many were eager to help, but the language barrier stopped it and many of the kids just wanted to touch the dark skin to see if it would rub off. I would joke and smile and say that color is not going anywhere. After a few minutes in the airport a Korean security guard escorted me to the USO and from there was able to get on a bus to Osan AB, Korea. After being there overnight the next day, I rode for three-plus hours to Pusan, Korea, which would be my home for the next year. This is shared because while living in Korea, this is the moment that I realized being what was an American. If there were adjectives that could explain what an American was in my eyes, it would be arrogant, privileged, entitled, blessed, unaware, egotistical, best, divisive, and honorable, to name a few. However, these are not the same words that would be used if I had to explain the black Americans in the United States. The realization that in America we were different; however, we were even more different in another country. Even though being in S. Korea as an ambassador of the US it was a rude awakening for me. In Korea, I started to realize who Clarence Jones was, was introduced to a life of loveless sex, and realized that I controlled more of my destiny than was realized before.

Many times, we do not know what we do not know. We do not realize why we do things and if we do things negative or positive, there are a lot of underlying issues that cause these issues. After ending my last relationship there was a realization that the common denominator in the situation was me. It was not until then that they realised that counseling could be an option or a need to get better. Counseling has always been something that was not popular to most black men or me. As a witness today, counseling is needed by everyone. There is nothing more freeing than to be able to tell your story, your truth, or your hurt without any judgement. Even though many times, I wonder how much the counselor tells her girlfriend or family about the nameless individuals they encounter. However, trusting the process to work is key. The only thing you can control is what effort you put into counseling so that you can receive just as much of the benefits of counseling.

The hardest part of counseling for me was reliving childhood and trying to figure out the real reason my marriage ended. Although there will never be an answer that I can get about the ending of marriage, having a safe space to speak, vent, cry and even curse about it was what was needed. Many times in life, when we think of childhood, we think of how we were raised, what was right and what was wrong in our mind about our life. Reliving my childhood to my counselor made me realize the reason that being an effective father was hard for me is that I was trying to give them what I missed instead of giving them what they needed at this specific time. Overall, counseling helped me realize the reasons behind my failures. It allowed me to take the little boy out of the closet that was put there in March of 1992 on the way to San Antonio, Texas. Freeing the little boy allowed him and me to be vulnerable, angry, bitter, and resentful. Most of all, counseling helped him heal and become friends with the man he had become.

Counseling is still hard to attend, but it's necessary. Many times, as black men, we think we can heal on our own and that is not the case. If you get the chance to go to counseling, you deserve to be whole, vulnerable, happy, and able to stand in your truth. Step outside of the box and into a world that is not so angry. Let counseling release the little boy so many of us are locked up.

CJ-ism# 18- *Fear is your insecurities telling your dreams/thoughts you cannot do it!*

HEALING

Chapter 7: Chasing the Ghost

Today, I am on a flight to Reno, NV. There are so many things going on in my mind as the navigation of my next career move is about to take place. One would say that there have been several career moves for me from the military up until now in the blood plasma and pharmaceutical company. There could be some agreement with the statement, but my belief is that the only thing that is a common denominator is what is or was being chased. Chasing the ghost is what it is called by me. Many of us have a ghost that we chase. In my case, this ghost is a success.

As I was outside playing in the yard, throwing rocks across the field from my house to my uncle's house, I was upset because I was left home, and everyone was gone except me, and I think my mom or sister was in the house. For some reason, at that age, I was contemplating what I would be when I grew up. There had always been the question in my head and every time from an early age, my main goal was to be a teacher. At this time, there was no description of what kind of teacher I would become; however, there was always the thought of being a teacher.

To tell the truth, I can't think of anything else that I wanted to be growing up. However, on this day, some of the specifics were vague, but I remember doubting myself. There was no reason that comes to mind, but remembering the doubt is very real. As I stood and looked over the hill to my uncle's house, there was a voice. It was an inner voice but I heard the voice externally also. The voice said, "You were not put here to fail." As I looked around there was no one outside but me. Again, the same voice said," You were not put here to fail." Now, it did not startle me, the voice did not scare me, and the voice caused me to be calm and at peace. It was almost as if there was a jolt of energy that reenergized me to throw more rocks. Many years would pass before this moment would be recollected, but even today, this moment in my life sustains me whenever there are times of doubt. In many cases, the remembrance of this voice is the only thing that has kept me from going crazy. Now that life has given me a few opportunities and a few lessons, the realization to me is that this voice is the beginning of my *Chasing the Ghost*.

At no point since this time has there ever been a moment that failing was an option. However, there are moments when I understand why people quit. In life, my belief is that your parents, either your mother or father, shape who you are in life. To me, this means that in life, you will either grow up trying to be like your mother or father in a good way or you will do everything in your power to be totally different. For me, it was the latter. Going to school was an adventure. Not because school was hard but because school was where you could be the cool kid today and the joke of the day tomorrow. Many times, what you wore determined which one you would be for the day. One night, my family and I were sitting in the house watching TV. It was a rare night that my dad was home earlier enough that we all were sitting down talking. My dad had a great sense of humor and when my mother and he was together, it was an in-house comedy show sometimes. On this night, it was clear my dad was singing a commercial that, at the time, we didn't know was a song. The commercial went, "I couldn't sleep at all last night. I was tossing and turning, turning, and tossing." The song would then fade out of the commercial. On this day, my dad was in the house, and he started to sing the whole song. It went, "I couldn't sleep at all last night. I was tossing and turning, turning, and tossing, I tossed, and I turned all night! I kicked the cover on the floor!" As a family, we died laughing, he had to sing the song at least five more times after that, which probably is the reason that it is still remembered to this day. It was sort of the perfect night, if you asked me, until I decided to ask the question that changed my way of thinking and aided me in my stubborn ways today. As we continued to watch TV, talk, and laugh, I asked my dad, can you buy me a pair of shoes? Out of nowhere, as if he was on cue, he said, "Didn't I buy you a pair of shoes last year?" the whole house laughed. They were not laughing at me. They were laughing at the point of how you can think that one pair of shoes that was purchased last year would somehow last a whole year. As everyone laughed, for me, it was one of my crying moments. I remember one of my siblings saying what did you think you were buying cowboy boots? It went on for about ten to fifteen minutes, but it felt like an eternity in my mind. This is one of the moments that made me realize that being successful is something that I had to be because, to me, success went hand in hand with money, and money meant that when it came to purchasing, what I could buy would not have a limit. "When I grow up, I will have enough clothes and shoes that I will not have to wear them more than once a month," is what I would say to my mother. She would just shake her head and say ok. Sometimes, she would say I know you want more clothes and shoes, but I just do not have it. It was understood, but at the time, that was all that I was looking forward to and being successful would do that for me.

The first time that success was tangible to me was in the military. In the military, you could receive your E-4 rank early if you won what was called *Senior Airman Below the Zone*. You would have to go in front of the leaders in the squadron and answer a few questions, get your uniform inspected, and they would test your military bearing. One would also have to be nominated for this by doing extra volunteer work or excelling at your job. The day had arrived, and it was time for me to go in. Everything went perfectly and when I left the room, there was a thought that no way was there anyone that could have done better than me. Every question was answered, the uniform was impeccable, and the military bearing and facing movement were crisp. "Give me my Stripe" is what I would joke with the guys. The same day, there was a room inspection in the dorm, the squadron commander was coming around to inspect rooms and the person had to be in the room when she visited. She entered my room and looked around and it was good to go. She said that she had heard that I went up for below-the-zone and she asked me how I think I did. Without hesitation, I said, "I think I got it!" Now that I looked back, she was asking how I did and I told her basically I won. Well, the next morning, she called me in her office, and she gave me my below-the-zone stripe. She said you told me yesterday that you had won, and she said congratulations, Airman Jones. Success was sweet, I liked the way it felt, I liked the way I was treated, I liked the attention, and I liked the competition. My ghost was moving, the chase was on and at this moment, we were neck to neck. It would only be years later that it was realized that chasing that ghost comes with consequences, a spotlight, a pedestal, and artificial friends and leaders who are waiting to knock the pedestal down.

Many times in life, we shape our own minds about what success looks like for us. This shape is formed by lifestyle, experiences, motivation, and where you spend most of your time. Money never shaped my success, but, in my mind, you could never have the money that you needed unless you were successful. What was never shared with me was the more money you make, the more money you want. With the increase of wants comes the growth in your mind of what your success should look like, not necessarily to you, but to the people around you. Many times, the question to myself has been, when did your definition of success change? There is a point in all our lives that we change our meaning of success for acceptance. Not the acceptance as wanting to be a friend. It is a change as to this is what society says is successful and if it is not obtained by me, then I have not reached the level of success that should satisfy me. Today, it is even more dangerous because the level of what is successful is instilled in many kids' minds at an early age. Most times, it only deals with material things. Navigating success by far has been the hardest thing for me in my lifetime. If I were to put my career up to many people as far as money made, education and training, people influenced, job status, and accomplishment, I would say that it would be considered way above average. The funny thing about it is that my level of success changed and because of what many consider successful as you change your environment, many people look back at their careers and think that nothing has been accomplished. Today, I can say that is me.

When I first enlisted in the military, there was no idea of how long I would stay or why am I in here besides to have my own money. Money again has been the catalyst of changing the ghost and moving the goal line of what is a success. After being in a few years, the goal became to make master sergeant, have a retirement ceremony where I could walk out to Encore by Jay-Z, influence people, and have enough money that I would not have to work if I did not want or have a house car and the picket fence in Franklinton, NC. Because this was not done for many years, in my mind, my military career was a complete failure. Not because I did not accomplish a lot but because of the idea of what was successful in the military I had not achieved. I shaped my ghost and chased it and could not catch it. Not until I started receiving calls from old troops and receiving letters of thanks from them, people calling asking for career advice, did I realize that sometimes success is going to be different for many people. If I look back on it, no, I did not make MSgt, but my influence and impact on people that I encountered in the military will stand the test of time against anyone who has served. There was no retirement ceremony. However, the dinner that my troops gave me and the emotions and words they spoke meant far more than someone, many of whom may not like me seeing me walk out to Jay-Z encore. However, one day, it will be used to march out to something. Even though at this moment I still must work, currently, I am in a position where not having to work is attainable and if there is something that I want or need, there is not question that it can be had. Overall the success of my military career does not look like the normal retired military person, but doing 20 years 14 days was a success, influencing people was a success, and being stable enough to support a family has been a success. It took me many years to realize that success is not determined by what people on the outside think of you but by how you influence and impact the people you encounter on your journey to being successful.

She said, "It ain't no fun when the rabbit got the gun." This is probably one of the truest and the funniest statements that has been heard in my lifetime. I remember it like it was yesterday, sitting in the office in Incirlik, Turkey and two of my troops going in on the jokes about me. Most times, it would be me with the laughs, but this day, they came prepared and fully loaded. When she paused the jokes to say, "It ain't no fun when the rabbit got the gun", it was the frosting on top of whatever delicious dessert that they were serving. However that statement still reigns true as a civilian in today's world of corporate America. Since being out of the military, there have not been many times that I have had a gun, but when I have had the gun, it makes me realize how much of a responsibility it is to actually shoot.

Chasing the Ghost, to me, is the unrealistic journey to achieve a level of success that will keep you satisfied and sustained in your everyday life. A feeling of fulfillment. What determines that fulfillment in your life? How will you know when you have succeeded in your level of fulfillment? Is it okay to never catch the ghost? What does catching the ghost mean? Is the ghost really you chasing life to get back the things that you have lost, insecurities, validation, family, disappointments, or acceptance? Is your ghost determined by man or self and if it's determined by you, why do you keep moving the goalpost.

My Uncle Jerdon was so special to me. It wasn't because he had great accomplishments or was profound in his speaking. He was special to me because to me, he had a calmness about him sometimes that said I am good here in my garden, singing "Sittin on the Dock of the Bay" by Otis Redding. We would talk and play checkers and most times, if I asked him for something and he had it, he would give it to me. Also, he would tell you when he did not want to do something and would stick by it. There were times when I would go to his house and he would say, I don't feel like dealing with anyone today and send me back home. As a young boy, I would think he is being an asshole, but as an adult, I see it as him not compromising his peace. How satisfied with life do you have to be that you are at peace and regardless of who or what it is that you will not compromise your peace to please someone else other than yourself? Could peace be the kryptonite to your ghost, internally and externally? All the questions asked are answered when one has peace.

As I continue to ride this plane to Reno, I people-watch, and it seems as if everyone has something on their mind. Not too many people seem as if they are at peace. It's the realization that everyone is chasing a ghost and that their ghost changes just like us all. I think and I realize that my ghost has me on this plane to Reno. A couple of months ago, my supervisor resigned. When he resigned, it left a major void in work and even the knowledge that he shared. He was a young man that is destined for success and in him sometimes I saw that he was also chasing a ghost. His eagerness, ambition, and energy reminded me of a younger me until this world and my decision caused me to turn bitter. Many days, I wanted to tell him to use me for questions on leadership and how to navigate through difficult people. However, we just worked and had some good moments as we traveled. When he left, I knew his job would have to be filled and with me being at the company for nine months, in my mind, I was thinking, it's no way they will let me have a manager's position this early. Besides, many of the people there would not even speak when you walked past them in the hallway, much less a manager. There was even a time when the director was told by me that the job was not a good fit for me at the time. Basically it was just a time when my insecurities were turning my doubts into fears. A fear that in my mind was not there, but subconsciously, it was because there was no way you deserve that, look where you come from, no black man is supposed to move up that quick, they will never have you in that position, the culture of Europe and you does not mix. All these things I was telling myself and then the voice came back that said, "You were not put here to fail." Immediately, the conversation in my mind turned to: You did the work, now reap the reward; You were not put here to fail; Do it for your haters (even though I do not know of any); and You are your ancestors' wildest dreams! This is what keeps me motivated. Five interviews were completed and there was minimal doubt that the job would be mine. However, at the time, trying to balance the two positions and trying not to give too much because they were only paying me as a Senior Supply Chain Analyst. One check, one job was my motto. While the wait was on, there were clues given that the job would be mine. Event to the point that it was told that the last step was to go to Spain and have the leadership team bless the hire. At this time, I knew that the only thing that would change would be the title because getting another person in to do my job would be in the next fiscal year. Get ahead of the power curve and if you have someone that you think would be a great fit, let them know was even told to me. This gave me even more confidence that the position would be for me. After waiting for a word from Spain that never came and no more talk of the job being mine, I asked what was going on. An email was received that said the manager position would be changed to a senior leadership position. Also, nothing else would happen until the new year. The disappointment was immediate. Not for me, but because there were people contacted with the possibility of getting a job and now my word was being compromised. The disappointment of the job did not sting as much because giving a big, cocky, black guy that does not shriek himself to make other people feel comfortable was not something that was done on a regular. To me, this would definitely not be done because senior leadership didn't speak when you looked them in the eyes, why do you think they will put you in as part of the leadership team? Besides, there was not one there now who looked like me, what made me special? I answered my own question: I did the work, I should reap the reward. I was not put here to fail, and why not me? This was my reason why and now it was time to decide how to respond?

As a black man, one of the hardest things to do is to balance who you are. Who do they say you are? What do you do? What do they think you are going to do? Regardless of what you do, you do not want to be the angry black man! That man I have never been, but because of my stature, it is not hard to convince people that you are not. Mentally, I was at war with quitting or continuing to do a job that I knew may not be granted to me. The battle in my mind was on, do I quit today and don't tell them anything or do I do my job because, at the end of the day it's not hard and you are getting paid decent money to do the job? The battle of how much I have to do to get accepted in corporate America. What other boxes do I have to check off? The education requirements MET. The job experience MET. The results-oriented resume MET. Everything needed, in my opinion, is met, except there is this hue on my skin that would not leave. Many times, I have been reminded of my time in Korea when the little kids would come up to me and touch my skin to see if it would come off. I would say, no, that is not going anywhere. This is what I was telling myself at this time, so a decision would need to be made. The color is not going anywhere and if I thought this was just an isolated incident, it is not (my previous experiences had confirmed that). The irony is that as I write, sitting here on the plane and going up to first class to use the restroom, the person beside me makes it his business to tell me that I do not belong up front to use the bathroom in first class. He says," You have to go to the back?" I say," Why do I have to go to the back?" "You are not first class," he said more emphatically. "Is it that you don't want me to go to the front or did they announce that I could not? The flight attendant had no problem," I told him. He just looks, and then I say, "Did you not want me to go to the front because you went to the back?" Awkward silence at this moment. This coincides with how I am feeling. Many times, there are people who don't want to be in places because either they have not been or they went a different route and feel you should do the same so that you do not have this preconceived advantage. Even though there are people we see every day who are getting a helping hand, there is a stigma by me and some black men that we must make sure we do or did the work and then be able to prove that we did the work if asked. So many times in places, there is a feeling of how you got here and who needs their floors cleaned. Chasing the ghost has put me at this point today. Sometimes, I think it can be close to an obsession. My ghost has all the answers or disproves all the things that bothered me in my life. My ghost holds counter to you are going to be just like your dad. My ghost holds the counter to you will never make it in the Air Force. My ghost holds the answer to you taking my stripe a few weeks from my retirement, knowing that the only thing it does is stop me from having a retirement ceremony. My ghost holds the counter with all the times I could not test to make rank, so my rank will be in corporate America where you can't stop me. My ghost does not have a DAMN thing to do with ME!

A ghost is defined as a disembodied soul. The soul of a dead person is believed to be an inhabitant of the unseen world or to appear to the living in bodily likeness. In the dictionary, the definition of chase is an earnest or frenzied seeking of something desired. So, for me, chasing the ghost has been seeking something that doesn't exist in this world. However, many people can see the ghost, is it there or what makes your ghost appear? For me, it has been a failure; the fear of failure has been my ghost and it has been covered or disguised as the pursuit of success. My ghost has consumed me, and it has challenged me in every aspect of my life. The need to chase this ghost remains, but at what cost? The cost of being a single father looking for love in a world where you will never be enough, but you do enough to survive. Chasing my ghost may not be worth it. I wish I would have learned before I lost so much.

CJ-ism #9 - *Some people are leaders, some people are followers, I just hate when the followers are put in leadership positions!*

Chapter 8. Finding Your Purpose

One of the differences between the military branches of the United States is that the Air Force prepares you to work in corporate America, while the other branches prepare you how to fight in corporate America. While transitioning from the military to the civilian sector my biggest transition was dealing with the lack of leadership and the lack of structure. The core values of the US Air Force are **Integrity First, Service Before Self, and Excellence in all we do!**

Since leaving the military, relying on these core values has been more of a staple now than it has been while in the military. In the military it is expected to live by the core values even though many do not. However, in the civilian sector, you will be lucky to get even one of these core values. Upon entering the civilian sector, for some reason, it was believed by me that this would be the norm. What a rude awakening. One of the biggest questions that I have asked myself is: What is my purpose? Now that the military is long gone from a career path, what my purpose is has become a daily question. Do I teach? Do I work? Do I go back to working for the government? Or Do I need to sit down somewhere and enjoy the fruits of my labor? Well, the latter will not happen or there will be very few fruits. Normally, trying to answer that question would have me trying every option that I could think and would come to mind. Through life challenges, I have learned that it is not what you become to the world but what and who you are as a man. While going through my self-evaluation and trying to figure out what would make me a good man, there were some things that can't be compromised if you want to be a well-rounded man or individual. I will explain them briefly, but the things a well-rounded man needs are Spirituality, Mental Stability, Stress Management, Communication Skills, Peace, and Self Care. Not everyone has all, and everyone has some, so if you are breathing, you are on your way to becoming a well-rounded man or individual.

Spirituality is something that a lot of people do not compromise, and they should not if it is your belief. When speaking of spirituality, the belief is that everyone should believe in something higher than themselves. We need to be aware of what drives our actions and emotions. How do we navigate our moral compass? In my opinion, everyone is born with morals. Morals are something that one can not teach. However, your morals are influenced by your spirituality or lack thereof. The definition of morals is a person's standards of behavior or beliefs concerning what is and is not acceptable for them to do. As stated prior, I firmly believe that everyone has time before any decision to make a choice. It is innate, no one just does something without having a choice in that matter before that action is complete. As a man, what do you stand on and believe governs how you run your life, how you run your household, and how you treat people, whether they are your family, friends, or associates? It is very obvious in my life when I know I have drifted spiritually. Decisions become reckless, anger becomes the norm, and doubt and hopelessness seep into my thinking. Drawing away spiritually dries up the human mind to think logically. It puts you in an emotionless desert and influences every aspect of your life. As men, we need to be grounded spiritually.

Spirituality, in my opinion, coincides with mental stability. In my experience, a lot of people that was not spiritually aware were also mentally challenged. Is it because I think my thinking is more logical than someone who is not spiritual or because being mentally stable also causes one to use logic and be logical? My biggest fight in relationships has been with mental stability. Coming home and sitting in the car to mentally prepare yourself to go home is a problem. As men, we think that some of these actions are normal and that is what every man goes through. One part of that is right and that is a lot of men go through those challenges. One of my most destructive sayings to the boys when we lived together was, "I am not here to be your friend. I am here to make sure I can trust you. If someone brings you to the door and accuses you of anything, I need to be able to trust you if you said you did not do it." The idea was correct, but my actions were flawed and mentally, it made sense to me because, as a man, I was instilling trust in young men with their parents. Now that time of reflection has happened, it may have been more mental damage than one expected. We always teach kids to make sure you have good friends, if you have good friends, you can trust that they will put you in a good situation and have your back at all costs. Having good friends caused your parents to be more comfortable letting you out of the house to do extracurricular activities. This is what we were teaching our kids. Good friends mean I can trust your actions was the lesson. However, at home, the father figure in the house was saying I am not here to be your friend, but I want you to trust me as you trust your friend. Do you want me to trust my friends, or do you want me to trust you, who tells me every day that I was not put here to be your friend? There is something mentally wrong with that scenario, but the kids were expected to believe it. Yes, it worked. I was not put here to be their friend, and, in my opinion, I was not considered a friend of theirs. Mental stability is very important because of the obstacles in the world. Wanting a pity party because being a black man is not something that I am looking for today. There is a lack of understanding of the mental challenges we face as a man. When my workday is over, there is not much thinking that goes on in my head. Not because it can happen, it's because, for most of the day, the internal battles that I face are exhausting. Every day, there is peace when I wake up. There is a prayer said for the people that I love and the people that hate me. I pray that if any fault was placed on an individual by me, knowingly or unknowingly for God to forgive me and to allow the person that was harmed or hurt to forgive me. Once the front door opens, there is mental instability that comes along with anxiety, anger, and determination. Immediately there is a mental picture taken of what needs to be done for the day. Always complete something during the day. Prioritize your day to be able to check off something you completed each day so that your day will not seem as if you did not complete anything. Driving to work most mornings, I thought of how long I was going to do this. Then the answer was as long as you have a daughter who thinks her parents are rich and she can get anything she wants, so forever. Once in the office, it starts. Do the right thing, CJ, "Good morning, how are you doing?" The shit-face smile is given and no words are spoken as people walk by you in the hall. This must be the most irritating thing that bothers me. The first decision comes, should I speak back to myself with the passive aggressive, good morning, CJ, I am well, I am glad that you are, or should I just let it go and count it as that is just the way they are until they speak to the next person in the hallway. As the day goes one deals with the scrutiny of everything that goes on when you are completing a project or deadline. As I was told by a director, that is just the culture; they shoot first, then aim. In my opinion, it's not culture; it's the thought that you are not supposed to be here where I am and most of my day is going to be trying to prove that you do not belong. It's sort of like going to the bathroom in first class every day. You are not supposed to be here. Finally, it is being overworked, but you try to complete everything because you must deal with the stereotypical thought of being lazy or the fight within of showing whoever doubts you that the hype is real and you belong where you are whether the other people like it or not. This is daily and it can affect everything for the rest of the day. That includes your family, communication, and mental health, which eventually starts to deteriorate your physical health. The mental wars that go on in our minds a lot of times go unchecked because of the machismo of sucking it up and moving on. It's part of being a man. In actuality, we are sick, and we need help managing our mental health.

"Hello, I am having chest pains. The pains are about an eight on a scale of 10. It started in my back, came down my left arm and now it's my chest. I took my blood pressure, and it was not high. This morning, it was 135/65, so it was pretty normal. My Apple Watch showed that I have been in atrial fibrillation since around lunchtime. I was sweating and took some Tylenol, but the pain would not subside," I said. This was the conversation that went on in the Emergency Room of the Veteran's Hospital every two weeks for nearly a year. After many trips, EKG, Stress Test, and MRI, the doctor said your heart is strong and there does not seem to be anything wrong with your heart. However, if what is stressing you out does not get better, there will be a problem. It is good that you come to the hospital when you are hurting, but eventually, you will continue to try to diagnose yourself and you will stop going to the hospital and with stress that one time you do not come will be the time that you need to come. You need to get the stressors out of your life before you have problems. According to the Sage Journals, higher levels of chronic stress, life stressors, and discrimination due to oppressive social and economic conditions are higher in black men. This has caused black men to have a greater risk of depression. Black men are 1.7

times more likely than white non-Hispanic men to have diabetes, according to The Richmond Magazine. It states that there is more cortisol produced in black men due to stress. They liken it to running from a bear or escaping a house fire. The cortisol levels begin high, but as the danger subsides, the cortisol level energy level subsides. In black men, due to socioeconomic stressors, the cortisol levels remain high all day as if you are being chased continuously. This causes depression, diabetes, and heart disease in black men at a higher rate than others. There must be a way for men and even women to relieve or manage stress. In order to manage my stress after the conversation, the decision was made in my mind that the situation would have to get better, or I would have to leave the situation. Choosing to leave the situation was one of the hardest but needed decisions that was ever made. Leaving my life, my four-year-old daughter still haunts me to this day. The thoughts of she will understand, she will forgive me, and how much trauma it caused her run through my mind daily. My thought on leaving was if moving to Raleigh would get me out of the stressful situation, then by the time the family was ready to move, we would have found a way to figure out how-to live-in a less stressful situation. There were a few issues from this thinking: one, it was not communicated properly by me in this situation and secondly, with retirement looming in the family, there were decisions that were not agreed on, and it felt that there was no say so or even consideration of my opinions. It is always in these situations that, in relationships, we think that we will figure it out. Not many times is there the thought that maybe we need help in figuring this out. After about two years of leaving, it was realized that the relationship would not work if we did not seek counseling and in my mind, there would be no going back if the couple's counseling was not considered. After the breakup and counseling, realizing that the thought of me being a single father sent me into a deep depression. Angry that one of my many goals in life was to break cycles. The cycle of being in a household without a mother and father, the cycle of being a single father with a baby mother. This is one reason that calling the mother of my child a baby mother hardly ever happens because she is way more than a baby momma, she is a helluva mother and, on good days, a great friend. However, the thought of waiting all these years to do it right or be on the path to being in the home daily with my daughter devastated me. On top of these thoughts, there was work stress. One of the things that, as a leader and manager, I wanted to do was give people opportunities. There would not be handouts, but if you were qualified for the position, reliable, and professional, then an opportunity would be yours. The goal was to build a team that allowed each of us to grow. My thinking is always that my job is to prepare you for the next position as a leader and mentor. However, the crew that was hand-picked and hired by me lost the trust or was influenced by an internal or external employee. "I make this look easy is something that is repeated if you ever work with me." It is said by me because, in my opinion stress is hidden very well, not always handled, and my brain functions better in the morning times. Most time at work, being there early is the normal activity for me. Many employees do not see how early that work is started. Many employees and management only see me speaking, smiling, and talking because knowing the people who work for you is important to me. Many do not realize that hours have been put in before one has stepped foot out of their bed. With this being done, I joke that "I make this look easy." Some do not realize that the work has been done and get the mindset that if they can do it, then there is no doubt in their mind that they can do it, too. They discount my experience, my dedication, my training, and education. They minimize and marginalize my qualifications to try to satisfy their egos. Trying to manage people who think they should be in your position is another stressor to go along with many day-to-day stressors that make life a living hell. The depression lasted for me for nearly three months. There was daily crying, constant sleeping, many arguments, and the daily face of smiles because pretending that everything was alright was a must. One of the things that surprised me about depression and my anger going through my depression was that I expected my close relatives and friends to realize that depression was happening. If they were more attentive and checked on me more, then they would know that there was a problem. It didn't happen and I resented them also. Stress had caused me to be a prisoner in my own home and to lose out on the only person that I felt loved me unconditionally and that was my daughter. Suicides amongst men are more successful because we go through more drastic means to carry them out. I say this to say suicide was never an option for me, but at this moment, it was realized and understood that if you are not mentally prepared or do not have the tools to cope with stress, this could happen. The voice that told me years ago that you were not put here to fail saved my life. Regardless of what happens in my life, failure is not an option, so coping with situations comes a little easier for me, but not always for other people.

Holidays are hard for everyone who is single and going through their own life challenges. As black men and men in general, we need to ask our friends questions and follow up. We need to put ourselves in their situations and sometimes do what we need to help them because, most of the time, we are not much different. One holiday there was a friend of mine, and he was going through a divorce.

Ironically, so was I, but it was not shared at this time. The holidays were coming around and with that being said, I invited my friends over for dinner, drinks, and laughs. He said he was not going to do anything, but I insisted that he come for a little while. He arrived early and we talked, and he was sort of surprised that the dinner was cooked by me. It was funny to him because he thought the body that I had was built by McDonald's. My other friends arrived, and we had a great time. After everyone left and he took a nap on the couch due to many drinks, we sat in the living room and talked. He said he was ok to drive and that he was about to leave but he wanted to thank me. "Oh, no problem," I spoke. "He said no I want to thank you for inviting and insisting that I come over." Okay, but at the time, it was normal for me, we were all away from families during the holiday time and what other way to spend it other than with friends? The he said, "If I had not come over to your house tonight and you had not insisted that I come, the plan was for me to kill myself tonight." I sat there in disbelief, we sat and talked and I hugged my brother and said if there is any time you need my help, ear, or even a place to get away from the silence, please let me know. Your life is too valuable to give up and this world needs you. I need you. I shared with him that I, too, was going through a divorce, and it was hard. The ironic thing was there were four of my friends, male and female, going through divorce and we didn't rely on each other as we should.

Many times, as men, we are going through the same struggles, but it's easier to hide them than to speak with your friends. Most of our stress comes from not sharing and becoming a ticking time bomb. Part of being a well-rounded man is we have to learn how to manage our stress. Stress leads to health issues, which leads to depression, which sometimes leads to suicide. We do not need to add to any other numbers. We need to learn how to manage stress and one of the ways to do this is to learn how to communicate the stress we have or are dealing with daily.

Communication is something that has been one of my weak points in becoming a well-rounded man. If a bet had to be placed, the bet would be placed that many of the men reading this book have or have had the same issue. Most of my problems have stemmed from the way that I communicate as a father, husband, partner, or friend or the way that I have been communicated to as the latter identities. Communication is the catalyst of things that are going to go right or wrong and if we do not know how to do it effectively nine times out of ten, we are going to get it wrong. Many think that men do not know how to communicate. This is something that causes disagreements in many conversations that I have had. It is firmly believed by me that most men stop communicating when they feel that they are not being heard. You do not get too many chances to ignore a man before we shut down and when we shut down, having us open back up may take an act of Congress. This is considered disrespectful, and it invalidates our opinion. Some of the experiences that caused me to be an ineffective communicator stemmed from being cut off while speaking, being ignored, and having your words turned into meanings that I did not intend. This, I had to learn was not always the other person's fault. For men, the easiest way from one point to another is a straight line. For some women, it is around the bend, over the river, and through the woods to grandma's house. Knowing this, one of the things that help me communicate more effectively is telling the why. Some people like to know the why. This comes from parenting, marriage, and communicating effectively at work. In the military, as a leader, I would say we can speak about anything, but if you are asked to do something, you need to do it first and then we can discuss it afterwards. Well, you can throw that out of the window in all situations now. We have to answer the why. This causes us as men to express ourselves more and it gives our audience more of an understanding as to our reasoning. Communicating is not something that has a blueprint for doing effectively because of the different situations. However, if we as men include our why and sometimes go around the bend, over the river, and through the woods, we may make many situations better by being better men.

Finally, find peace and take care of yourself. Self-care is vital to a man's survival. This includes everything from male grooming, male me time, and spending time with the brotherhood. We cannot survive in this world alone and we must seek out someone of the same sex to sharpen our thoughts and our thinking and to express our emotions. We all need "Am I Crazy or What?" moments with the guys. Self-care includes finding guys or a guy you can trust so that you can be vulnerable in all situations. One of the most vulnerable moments that I have experienced is when I had to tell my friend, I missed my family and, in my mind, there is uncertainty if the right decision was made. Through conversation, I learned that sometimes tough decisions take us away from the ones we love. However, it may be easier to be away from the situation instead of being dead because of the situation. Self-care is like a tune-up for men that engages all aspects of being a well-rounded man spiritually and mentally, relieving stress, communicating, and living a balanced life of peace and family.

For years, trying to finish this book has been a struggle. Not because it made me vulnerable but because it was therapy. There are so many chapters on the floor that did not make the book and those chapters were not meant to make the book. They were to help me on my journey to becoming a well-rounded and better man. This is a conversation piece that can be discussed or even start discussions for us as men. *First to Finish; Last to Win* is about the race that we go through every day in life. Many times, we just want to finish, and the win is not even important. However, winning makes it a little bit more satisfying.

CJ-ism #14 - *In life, we make decisions, a lot of times, we look back and say well, I should have done this, or I could have done that. We overlook one of the most important parts of the situation. The most important thing is that "YOU MADE A DECISION." We are never going to get everything right but be brave or have enough faith to make the DECISION!*

Chapter 9: CJ-isms – The List

1. CJ-ism #1 - Just because you are talking does not mean anyone is listening!
2. CJ-ism #2 - When life hits you in the mouth, keep smiling... Life can't knock those teeth out again!
3. CJ-ism #3 - When you think what you do isn't enough, stop worrying about what other people think!
4. CJ-ism #4 - If you wake up in the morning, and don't see someone you love, go back to bed, it's not even work starting the day!
5. CJ-ism #5 - If my status page shows 16 posts and over half of them are yours, you may need to cut down on the posts!
6. CJ-ism #6 - When you become so emotionally involved with a situation or subject that it starts to make you treat people like you never treated them before, it may be time to self-evaluate!
7. CJ-ism #7 - People that just talk to hear themselves talk, should have to wear earphones to hear themselves constantly.
8. CJ-ism #8 - No Words... I just want to tell my sisters "I LOVE THEM" Janet, Lisa, Ann, & Vanessa.

9. CJ-ism #9 - Some people are leaders, some people are followers, I just hate when the followers are put in leadership positions!
10. CJ-ism #10 - Real friends tell you what you need to hear and not what you want to hear. So if your friends have never told you anything bad, they may not be your friends, or you are Perfect!
11. CJ-ism #11 - When we get people who try to discount what we have been through as unimportant and they say that it doesn't matter anymore, we began to lose ourselves. When you say the past that has shaped you doesn't matter, you become lost. There is nothing worse than a man that will not "acknowledge" his past and act as if his past never happened.
12. CJ-ism #12 - Character is not someone that is in a movie, and if you think so, go find yours!
13. CJ-ism #13 - Stop talking and say something!
14. CJ-ism #14 - In life, we make decisions, a lot of times, we look back and say well, I should have done this, or I could have done that. We overlook one of the most important parts of the situation. The most important thing is that "YOU MADE A DECISION." We are never going to get everything right but be brave or have enough faith to make the DECISION!
15. CJ-ism #15 - Thank God for the hard times...
16. CJ-ism #16 - We must die daily to live forever!

17. CJ-ism #17 - I wasn't put here to fail, IT'S NOT AN OPTION!

18. CJ-ism #18 - Fear is your insecurities telling your dreams/thoughts you cannot do it!

19. CJ-ism #19 - Just because you do not wear glasses does not mean that you are not blind!

20. CJ-ism #20 - MARRIAGE consist of three things... COMMUNICATION, DEDICATION, AND FOUNDATION! Communicate your feelings, be dedicated to each other & build a foundation. 6 yrs. have been a blessing, because of CD&F, we survived. Nothing has been easy. I thank my WIFE for communicating when I was stubborn, dedicated when I'm unlikeable, and building a marriage on GOD! I celebrate MARRIAGE! My Wife, Myself, & God... W/O him, there is no US!

21. CJ-ism #21 - Something to think about... Men are well aware that as the "HEAD OF THE HOUSEHOLD" nothing comes in our homes except through US?... a lot to swallow, but think about things that happen at home and then think about what we do or are doing and how it has an impact...INTERESTING.

22. CJ-ism #22 - Not until men stop seeing showing emotions as a sign of weakness will we ever be able to love our women the way they supposed to be loved!

23. CJ-ism #23 - Respect - why do we look for respect from people that we do not know, when the most influential people in our lives give it to us and we ignore it!

24. CJ-ism #24 - Sometimes we take for granted what we say and how it influences or inspire other people. We minimize our words as everyday thoughts of no significance, but when you speak the truth and from the heart, your words become light for people in darkness. How much light are you spreading?

25. CJ-ism #25 - Sometimes we don't realize that the shoes we wear are much bigger than what the size says!

26. CJ-ism #26 - Some of the hardest wounds to heal are the wounds without scars!

27. CJ-ism #27 - If you were to lose everything materialistic today, would you still be happy or have joy? Do material things run your life? Growing up I said when I was grown that I would have enough clothes to wear something and not have to wear it again for two months now that I have it. I wear the same thing over and over... How ironic!

28. CJ-ism #28 - What we think is important in life really isn't, but when we find out, it's too late. Time to Re-evaluate!

29. CJ-ism #29 - You may be small in man's eye, but you are a giant in God's eye. This world is too small, there is nothing that you cannot conquer!

30. CJ-ism #30 - P.R.I.D.E... Playing Righteous in Destructive Expectations!

31. CJ-ism #31 - When I grow up... I want it to be time to die! Enjoy life, live it to the fullest.

32. CJ-ism #32 - If one door closes, another one will open, but if you were too slow for the first one, you may need to change some things in your life, you may miss the next one also.

33. CJ-ism #33 - It's easy to listen when you do not have to; it's hard to listen when you need to.

34. CJ-ism #34 - Someone always sacrifice for you to succeed, who are you sacrificing for...

35. CJ-ism #35 - Imagine if you controlled all of time. How long would an hour or year be to u? Sometimes, we think we wait too long. In God's eyes, we are not waiting long at all. Stop looking at things in the right now and start looking at the right when... Right when u need it, God is on time. His timing is perfect. BE PATIENT!!

36. CJ-ism #36 - Is keeping it 100 the new keeping it real? And at that moment where you are keeping it 100: what were you before then 90, 50, 10...

37. CJ-ism #37 - Your journey is your story; you can change it to your liking. So, if you are in a situation, change the story.

38. CJ-ism #38 - You are more than you are worth! Many times, we say we cannot be bought, but when we settle, it is the same as being bought. YOU ARE MORE THAN YOU ARE WORTH. So, what have you settled and sold yourself for?

39. CJ-ism #39 - Giving up – Not an option, Giving out – A possibility, Winning – Always within reach!

40. CJ-ism #40 - Sometimes you keep fighting and fighting and you want to give up because you are tired of fighting. With all fighters you think this next punch could be the knockout, so you swing one more time. Keep swinging one punch at a time, you may get hit more, but eventually you are going to get your knockout. So your fight may slow down, but don't give up. Swing for the fences one punch at a time.

41. CJ-Ism #41 - Reality is never real, until it hits home.

42. CJ-ism #42 - Your situation is not your life!

43. CJ-ism #43 - Why Me? Why not you? Have you realized that you will not be given more than you can handle. So instead of asking, why me? Ask, why not me? Go through the struggle to get the prize because your reward is going to be a blessing to you and others. So Why Not Me? Because God knows you can handle it. Embrace the struggle and live!

44. CJ-ism #44 - Never compromise who you are for what you do.

45. CJ-ism #45 - Every situation we are in is because of a decision we have made directly or indirectly. So what we should do is to blame ourselves, forgive ourselves, and fix the situation. You can't fix your situation without forgiving yourself for making the decision.

46. CJ-ism #46 - Some mistakes lead to experiences; just remember some experiences we do not need to experience.

47. CJ-ism #47 - Everyone is there to help you make the decision, but no one is there to help you through the decision!

48. CJ-ism #48 - It is easy being consistent in doing things. The problem comes when you are not consistent in being YOU!

49. CJ-ism #49 - However, Hallelujah! However you get through the day, give Him the highest praise!

50. CJ-ism #50 - Destruction does not happen from a group of small events. Destruction happens from not taking care of the "Main Event" ... YOU!

51. CJ-ism #51 - Before you bring up my past, acknowledge my present. If you are still living in my past, you must not be in my present. Do not try to take me where I left you.

About the Author

Clarence Jones grew up in Franklinton, North Carolina the youngest of ten children. He served 20 years in the U.S. Air Force, after 20 years of service and he completed his education with a BS in Supply Chain and Logistics and a MS in Human Resource Strategic Management. He returned to civilian life and began his career as a supply chain and logistics professional. As a mentor, leader, husband, father, son, winner, loser, and black man in America, he felt it was time to share his experiences and life lessons in his publishing of "First to Finish, Last to Win."